Harvest of Bittersweet

Patricia Penton Leimbach

Illustrations by Jack Homesley

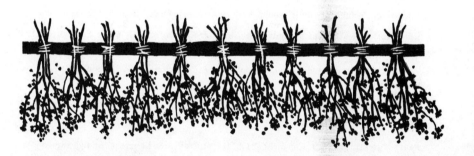

1817

HARPER & ROW, PUBLISHERS, New York

Cambridge, Philadelphia, San Francisco, Washington
London, Mexico City, São Paulo, Singapore, Sydney

Portions of this work originally appeared in the Elyria *Chronicle-Telegram*.

Grateful acknowledgment is made for permission to reprint:

Lines from "A Standing Ground" in *Farming: A Hand Book*, copyright © 1970 by Wendell Berry. Reprinted by permission of Harcourt Brace Jovanovich, Inc.

Lines from "For August" by Eileen Black. Reprinted by permission.

Excerpt from "Joy and Sorrow" reprinted from *The Prophet*, by Kahlil Gibran, by permission of Alfred A. Knopf, Inc. Copyright 1923 by Kahlil Gibran and renewed 1951 by Administrators C.T.A. of the Kahlil Gibran Estate and Mary G. Gibran.

Lines from "The Lent Lily" from "A Shropshire Lad"—Authorized Edition—from *The Collected Poems of A. E. Housman*, copyright 1939, 1940, © 1965 by Holt, Rinehart and Winston, Publishers; The Society of Authors as the literary representative of the Estate of A. E. Housman; and Jonathan Cape Ltd., publishers of *A. E. Housman's Collected Poems*.

Lines from "Winter at Bellside" copyright © 1964 by Mary Oliver. Reprinted by permission.

Lines from "Two Tramps in Mud Time" from *The Complete Poems of Robert Frost*, copyright 1930, 1949 by Holt, Rinehart and Winston, Inc. Reprinted by permission.

"March Night" by Mary Jean Irion, first published in *The Literary Review*. Reprinted by permission of Mary Jean Irion.

Lines from "Oversonnet" by David McCord. Reprinted from *The New Yorker Book of Verse*, copyright 1935 by Harcourt Brace Jovanovich. Reprinted by permission.

FIRST EDITION

Designer: Erich Hobbing
Copyeditor: Karen McDermott

Library of Congress Cataloging-in-Publication Data

Leimbach, Patricia Penton, date
   Harvest of bittersweet.
   1. Farm life—Ohio—Vermilion. 2. Lembach,
Patricia Penton, 1927– . I. Title.
S521.5.03L45   1987   630'.9771'22   86-46080
ISBN 0-06-015729-1

87 88 89 90 91 RRD 10 9 8 7 6 5 4 3 2 1

For Orrin, who brought us into the computer age with the production of this book; for Paul, who enables and endures; for my sister Mary Alice, who through the years continues to protect, encourage, scold, and lend her loving hands

Contents

Autumn

Winter

Autumn

Winter

Foreword

Selling bittersweet was one of the pocket-money enterprises my brothers and I pursued as farm children in the thirties. Through August and September we charted the hedgerows and the wildwood where it grew in chartreuse profusion. When autumn mellowed into Indian summer and the berries fattened, we cut the tangled vines, stuffed them in gunnysacks, and lugged them home to the loft above the cider mill. During the fall evenings we stripped the leaves, trimmed the stubborn, twisted strands into lengths for bunching, and hung them on a wire to ripen. Mother then wrapped the bunches in newspaper and sold them at the farmers' market in Lakewood, a western suburb of Cleveland, along with her apples and cider and cottage cheese. "Make a little space at the back for the children's bittersweet," I hear her saying to the older boys as they loaded the truck for market on Friday nights.

In later years, when I was a student at the university on Cleveland's east side, Mother would take a streetcar across town at the end of a market Saturday in October, toting a peck of apples, a half-gallon of cider, and a small bunch of bittersweet to brighten my dorm room. As the red-orange berries gathered dust in a blue bowl on my radiator through the winter, they were a talisman against homesickness, evoking thoughts of Mother, sister Mary, and the boys, of Penton Orchards and home, and of our genial childhood.

Bittersweet no longer flourishes in the fencerows as it once did, but I find no shortage of it in the real harvest of my life, a life that has involved me, through my earlier books and a chance career as a public speaker, with farm people all across the United States and Canada. I have gathered for you here some memories mingling, inevitably, the bitter and the sweet.

I hope these essays will summon for each of you private reveries—humorous, sad, nostalgic, but warm and bright and satisfying . . . like bittersweet. I am pleased that you would make a little space for them.

Spring

'Tis spring; come out to ramble
The hilly brakes around,
For under thorn and bramble
About the hollow ground
The primroses are found.

—A. E. Housman,
"The Lent Lily"

Meadow Ghosts

On the first warm day everybody is entitled to roll down the convert-
ible top of his mind and let the breeze ruffle his hair, to follow
meandering water and pursue the dreams of winter. Out the door,
across the yard, and past the barn. . . . The springs are running from
the hillsides, the water collecting in small grassy pools and slowly
seeping riverward.

In the irrigation pond below the hill, water is trickling into the
overflow pipe and leaking on down the spillway. I scare up a pair of
mallards, who fly off in ballet formation. Humans could learn a lot
about marital harmony from that pair.

A young turtle is pulled up like a skiff on the bank, sunning himself, stretching his neck about, unmindful of my intrusion. I seat
myself on a fallen log and wait for him to do something—to retreat or
retract or plod on up the bank.

There is an age that belongs to meadow ponds, that time in life
much occupied with exploration and discovery. More than any other
place on the farm, this was the kingdom where the children reigned.
I miss a little boy with wonder on his face and mischief lurking

3

behind his eyes—like brother John's son Jeffrey, whose spirit is everywhere around this pond. It was Jeffrey who named it "the turtle pond" to distinguish it from the three other ponds scattered about the place. He came to End o' Way at age four and a half, when his mother died, and stayed till he was seven and a half, perhaps the best three years in a boy's life. He remains a legend here for his skill at catching frogs. They brought home fists and pockets and buckets full of frogs, he and Dane, our firstborn.

"How do you do it, Jeff?" I asked him.

"Ya just sneak up behind 'em and grab 'em," he'd say, but nobody else could do it.

My turtle, moved suddenly by some voice of his own perception, plopped into the water and I missed the whole maneuver. I was looking across the sunlit ripples, remembering Dane at five fishing there in red rubber boots with a happy grandfather.

Among the debris caught in the cattails at the water's edge floats a splintered canoe paddle, relic of endless summers of little kids with rafts and boats. A young Teddy would have waded boldly in to retrieve it and been soaked in the process. It was a beckoning day like this one when Tammy Pritchett fell off the dock and nine-year-old Ted jumped in to pull her out, establishing himself locally as god to little girls.

A fallen cottonwood, long dead, bridges a deep gully that erodes the valley wall. Like the turtle, the pond, and the paddle, it invites a child's mischief. But the children are gone.

Sloshing toward the woods from the spongy end of the pond, I pass through six bedraggled acres of soybeans claimed by an early winter. Hoof prints here and there are a sign that the deer at least made a healthy harvest.

I note with a vengeful eye that a woodchuck hole midfield is flooded. If I were that long-ago Teddy, I would measure its depth with my boot or at least poke in there with that splintered canoe paddle.

A few strands of rusted barbed wire at the ends of the rows aim to keep the wild blackberries in the pasture and the soybeans up on the hill. The woodchuck and deer suffer no inconvenience from it, surely. No more did the small motorcyclists in their day. Now even the old trails about which we raised such cries of despair are nearly overgrown. My motorcyclists too have gone on to trails of greater glory. How the meadows are haunted today.

I find a rock above the spring and settle myself to read again

Wordsworth's "Lines" on nature composed above Tintern Abbey. At fifty I begin to relate to his twenty-eight-year-old wisdom, but it does not dispel the melancholy of little boys lost.

The short way home is up across the rye field, thick and springy underfoot. Heidi, my Lab, appears at the brow of the hill and comes wagging happily toward me. And there in the blue above the rye is that pair of mallards, still moving in rhythmic symmetry. But no . . . it isn't a pair of mallards at all. It's a box kite! Lifting and dipping, and lifting again.

And anchored to it, all that's left to us of "little boy"—Orrin. Even at this distance I can see the essential detail a mother's eye is conditioned to note: he hasn't changed his school clothes. The kite suddenly plummets, crashes, and he works at repairs while I approach to help him rewind the kite string.

Do you tell a kid of seventeen to go change his clothes? Not, I think, when he appears as an intimation of immortality.

Manual Training

When Fred sticks his head in the door and hollers "Honey, are you busy?" well, brace yourself. It's a leading question, and you can bet your sweet life it's going to lead you a long way from the morning's agenda. Make no mistake about it, there is nothing a farm wife does that's more important than what her husband does.

There's a myth passed from mother to daughter to granddaughter that once upon a time a woman snapped back, "You're doggone right I'm busy." She's now eking out a living braiding rugs of plastic breadwrappers at a flea market in the Ozarks. No farm woman, of course, believes she actually said that.

When you have assured him that you have nothing to do this morning but trip around in your negligee dusting the plants, he'll come in, lay his grimy gloves on the counter, push back his cap, and say, "I want you to run into town for me." You might as well punch down the bread and shove it in the refrigerator because your morning is shot. You're headed into town for a part, but there's no guarantee that you won't end up in Moline, Illinois.

If the parts man is skulking under the counter when you come struggling in with the "hickey" you want replaced, you may judge that somebody saw you coming. "Oh Lord, it's Clarabelle again!"

There is a natural animosity that exists between a farm wife and a parts man. These guys have been sadistically trained to trip you up.

By golly, you'll snap his garter this time. You've got this great big greasy doohickus here wrapped in an old afghan, and you plunk it down smugly on the counter in front of him. "I want one just like that."

"What kinda tractor'd it come off of?"

"Well . . . it's green."

"Swell. All our tractors are green."

"The tires come up to about here."

"Lady, that don't tell me nothing. I need a number."

"But I've got the part right here."

"It don't do no good. They've discontinued that part."

"Oh boy. Maybe you could show me some pictures. I'd know it if I saw it."

"I'll bet." He rummages about in the file and comes out with some brochures. "Any a them?"

"Oh dear. They all look alike, don't they?"

"Maybe if you'd just tell me which side of the tractor it fits on, that'd help."

"Oh sure! The side next to the barn."

The parts man rolls his eyes heavenward and says, "Tell you what, lady, why don't you call your husband and ask him what this thing came off of?"

If you're lucky you get Fred on the CB, or you reach a neighbor who sends the feed man out to the place where Fred's got the tractor torn down.

"He told the feed man to tell me to tell you not to forget the bolt," the neighbor adds when the tractor has been identified.

"Oh yes, I want a carriage bolt."

"How long?" says he.

"The exact distance from my knuckle to the end of my thumbnail." The parts man shakes his head and wonders why he ever gave up his job pumping gas. It seems a perfectly logical measurement to a woman who's accustomed to measuring yard goods from the tip of her nose to the end of her outstretched hand.

"And while I'm here, I want one of those round things with a hole in it."

"Lady, I got 10,000 parts here and half of them are round and got a hole in them."

"Well, it goes around and you put a rope over it."

"You mean a pulley?"

"That's it, a pulley!"

The longer you stay at this business, the smarter you get. You learn to go fortified with names, numbers, parts manuals, parts, adjacent parts. And if you're really on the ball, you go out and see exactly where and how the old part fits into the scheme of things.

There comes a day when, by golly, you KNOW you've got it all together. You stride confidently into the dealer's, you look the parts man squarely in the eye and give him the whole nine yards.

"I want a breakaway coupling for a ten-foot hydraulic hose with a half-inch pipe thread number 0029H53 that fits on a Ford 3000."

But it's no use. These parts men spend their weekends poring through parts books, searching for ways to confound you. They lie sleepless in their beds at night plotting, scheming, dreaming up questions that will defeat you.

"Do you want a male or a female plug?"

"I'll tell you what, fella. Just give me one of each and I'll go home and raise my own."

Toad and Me

When I dream the ultimate dream of happiness, it is a warm spring morning and I am at the wheel of some snappy little car headed south on the open road with only a vague idea of a destination and no scheduled agenda.

In these moments of reverie, I recognize my peculiar kinship to Mr. Toad of *Wind in the Willows* fame, whose life was transformed— well-nigh destroyed—by his discovery of and subsequent addiction to the motor car.

I am always alone in these dreams, and there is a logical explanation. For one thing, I have grown accustomed to my own company through the past ten years of traveling, and I find that conversation distracts me from full concentration on the pleasures of driving and the details of the scenery.

My intimate friends contend, however, that I simply don't like people sitting there white-knuckled, catching their breath at the top of every rise in the roadway (as people are prone to do when they ride with me).

Why am I going south? Perhaps because we Northerners have come to recognize south as the direction of sun and surf and endless summer. But the direction really doesn't matter.

Just give me a road—a straight road through flat farm country that laces together a parade of villages dominated by grain elevators and water towers, lumberyards and farm supply stores. A rippling road that winds among green hills where cattle graze and silos sidle up to dairy barns.

Or give me a shady back road through wasteland where marshy ground has grown up into woodlots and forgotten fences are hidden in a tangle of blackberry. I like a road that runs along an abandoned railroad bed where kids on trail bikes will not let the sumac forget that this is still a thoroughfare.

A high road along a mountain ridge is my favorite, sashaying past country churches and abandoned houses where lilac and forsythia remember, dipping and curving, plummeting into a valley to race side by side with a rocky stream.

I don't think of a car trip as a monotony to fill the space between coffee breaks and lunches. I just like car trips for their own sake. But I am not averse to slamming on the brakes and backing up for something that bears examination. I love a church that appears to be taller than the grain elevator and will detour down the side street that leads to it.

Shady cemeteries on hillsides at the end of long lanes are nearly irresistible. My favorite to date is one south of Petersburg, Illinois, where I found the grave of Nancy Hanks just a few paces from that of Edgar Lee Masters.

I like the little signs at side roads that beckon one to places such as Clover Bottom and Goodnight, Gravel Switch and Blue Moon. Sometimes you just have to go look! I am a sucker for people's birthplaces—on one brief trip in Missouri, I found those of both Jesse James and John J. Pershing.

In just one of those glorious vagabonding weeks I logged 1,200 miles through three states, with the wind blowing my hair and the radio tuned full pitch to country western. Of course, the trip had destinations and agendas, but I have a talent for making both a little vague. Mr. Toad would have been proud.

Mountain Mama

Between the shrink-wrapped cards of combs, key chains, and pipe cleaners in the general store at Deerwalk, West Virginia, hangs a poster announcing, "Four-Wheel-Drive Pull and Turkey Shoot over to Butcher Bend . . ." on a coming Saturday. Now that may not sound earthshaking, but it's the kind of news that catches the eye of the West Virginian who stops by "the store" for gas and coal oil, milk and Pepsi, cigarettes and bologna, and sends him away feeling that he got more than his money's worth. It's also the sort of local color that makes every exile homesick for West Virginia.

The couple who run the general store in Follansbee told me they once migrated to Akron, Ohio. "We couldn't stand it—all the hustle and bustle, being cooped up in a factory, day in, day out. We packed up and came back. Bought the store. Like to build a new place and expand, but times are rough. . . ."

I hope they don't. They might lose some of the atmosphere and that wonderful mélange of smells that endeared to me the old brick store on the corner alongside the creek in Follansbee.

"If you're going through Beckley," said my friend Ella once when we were traveling down to Bluefield, "you have to stop and see my mama." So we stopped to visit Mama and Aunt Cordy, Aunt Rainey, Uncle Scotty, and Uncle Verlan, brothers and sisters widowed and retired, resuming a communal existence in a big comfortable house on a sloping street in Beckley. They passed their time visiting friends in hospitals and rest homes, playing pinochle, attending funerals, and reminiscing about the good old days when they were young in Odd, West Virginia. They took us in and fed us, would have put us up for the month if we'd agreed. That's the sort of folks you find in West Virginia: super-friendly and laid back.

Just knowing a few West Virginians made me strangely homesick for its far-flung rural communities even before I'd ever been there. One autumn the Extension Homemakers invited me to speak for them down at the state 4-H center in Jackson's Mill. It's a handsome collection of stone cottages and meeting halls located at the boyhood home of Stonewall Jackson. The Homemakers must have sensed my kinship with them, for they have invited me back often since.

"Almost heaven, West Virginia, Blue Ridge Mountains, Shenandoah River . . ." but surely it's the country roads that do the most to win you to the Mountain State. You can speed through on a four-lane, but you'll only get fleeting glimpses of what life is like between the ridges, beyond the steeples, down in the valleys. "Life is old here, older than the trees, younger than the mountains, blowin' like a breeze."

A lot of these little roads are referred to as runs. The dictionary gives 172 definitions for "run," but not a one of them accurately describes a West Virginia run. "The beaten track or usual trail used by wild animals . . . a small stream, brook . . . a continuous extent of something. . . ." I took a detour up Tanner's Run and found it to be the beaten track along a small stream that probably extended to the hamlet of Tanner. I didn't hang in there long enough to find out for sure. When it crossed the creek, narrowed, and turned into dirt, I headed back to the blacktop. (The inner secrets of West Virginia are not for the faint of heart.) Tanner's Run was a peaceful little valley with a sprinkling of well-kept homes and more than one freshly painted porch with beckoning porch swing. I wound on then in the direction of Burnt House, Thursday, Alum Bridge, and Pickle Street.

Just reading the road map in West Virginia is a delight. You can easily tell that for most of its history it has been a remote and isolated outpost. More than in most states, the names tell the story, call a spade a spade: Flatwoods, Blandville, Stumptown, Looneyville, Mud. There's a fair share of place names for the Scotch, Irish, and English who settled this state because they found these highlands to be reminiscent of home. And a lot of respected matriarchs seem to have left their mark: Shirley, Idamay, Chloe, Hazelgreen, and Jane Lew among them.

At one point I climbed a steep driveway to a little clapboard Methodist chapel, peeked in the windows, walked back to the cemetery flowing down the hillside, and looked across the mountains, ridge upon ridge. Up in the industrial cities of northern Ohio, they tell the story of a guy who died, went to heaven, and found there to his surprise a sad soul chained to the pearly gate. "Why in heaven would you chain anybody?" he asked St. Peter.

"Have to," said St. Pete. "That fellow's from West Virginia. If we didn't chain him, he'd go home every weekend."

Can't say I'd blame him.

Conflagration Convocation

I stopped on Monday to see if Bev Schmalz's cats had come home. It was the cats who had alerted her to the barn's burning. She had seen the smoke when she went out to feed them, and as she ran to sound the alarm, the cats were scampering in the direction of the smoke.

Schmalz's barn was a dominant landmark in Rugby,* standing as it did on the ridge at the juncture of Bank Street and Morse Road just up the hill from the red brick, one-room schoolhouse. For more than a century it had watched the demise of the once-thriving village whose commerce centered in the gristmill on the Vermilion River below. Schmalz's barn was the convenient hangout for the neighborhood kids, who played basketball, cops n' robbers, or kick-the-can or just languished in the diminishing light of late summer evenings, shooting the breeze, planning great futures.

The township road crew had convened with their machinery on the oval before the barn to plot the day's activity, waiting for a tank of road oil or a load of slag. (One or the other of the Schmalz brothers has been a township trustee for a couple of decades.)

In other years Russell had raised a ten-foot star above the barn and silos at Christmas that could be seen for three or four miles east and west of the valley. Rugbyites knew we were homing where that star loomed. Saturday it was billows of smoke that beckoned.

Bev rushed to the house, called the fire department, and alerted her nephew John, working nearby. Then, running to the field behind the barn, she waved her red bandana to summon her husband and her brother-in-law, whose attention was riveted on their corn planting.

In that five-minute interval the smoke had erupted in flames that filled the barn cavity. John had removed the grain truck and his own car. Charles and Russell came running, but haste was futile by then.

Up at End o' Way Paul spied the blaze from where he and Orrin were planting potatoes. "Schmalz's barn's on fire!" They unhooked the planter and Paul sped down the road with the Farmall, thinking there would be machinery to tow. Orrin ran home for a second tractor.

By now the siding was nearly gone, and the slate roof hung

---

* Rugby is the Leimbachs' immediate neighborhood and derives its name from one of the seven school districts that originally constituted Brownhelm Township, our immediate neighborhood.

11

strangely above a rectangle of orange flame. An adjacent shed had collapsed, and the blaze threatened the grain bins and the drying shed with its expensive equipment.

The fire trucks, their sirens tapering off, glided in behind the drying shed, as Paul hooked his tractor to a lime spreader and pulled it to safety. The firemen unwrapped their hoses and began dousing the scorched grain silos. There was a near-audible sigh of relief from the neighbors, who were by now all there—the Frimels, Niggles, Pritchetts, Walkers, Murpheys, Dlugoses, Stoviceks, Clines—the same crowd who share our picnics, weddings, graduations, funerals.

A burning barn rates right up there with a farm sale or a church social for drawing a crowd. On this warm spring Saturday folks from four townships converged on Rugby, each noting with relief as he approached that the smoke was not anchored in his own piece of real estate, looking on then in morbid fascination and with a sense of frustration. We all yearn to be the hero who can reverse a calamity.

A second fire company arrived with two more pumpers, a tanker, and a hook-and-ladder truck. The county sheriff and the Vermilion police came with their red flashers glowing. Orrin busied himself keeping the road clear of traffic for the trucks shuttling to town for water.

Charles and Russell leaned against their machine shop and watched helplessly, an agonizing posture. They didn't need this with grain prices at a ten-year low. Time was at a premium. It was the onset of planting, and the spring supplies were in. Just yesterday they'd taken delivery of $16,000 worth of chemicals and stowed them in the barn. They hadn't been able to rescue their backhoe or the new fertilizer spreader. "Never been used," said Russell glumly.

Insurance? Well, you never know what's covered.

Just then there was a sharp crackling, and the roof collapsed. The vertical beams on the north side fell sideways into the yard.

"We just talked the other day about how we'd re-side it when we had a little extra money," said Charles' wife, Betty.

"Well, no lives were lost, and that's a blessing," said Bev. "Gee, I wonder what became of my cats."

A barn's burning is a fact farmers live with. You hear it in rural conversation: ". . . the year the barn burned." I tick them off in my head—the Baumans, the Borns, the Fowells, the Gedes, the Bauses, the Bob Leimbachs, the Shrivers—they all lost their barns.

We lost ours when I was a child. It seemed like the end of the world. I remember the scene of dejection in our kitchen that night.

Mayor Cooper drove his black Packard out from town, sat on a too-small chair holding his hat against his ample stomach, and apologized that the fire department hadn't been able to do much.

Something there is that doesn't love a barn, to borrow from Robert Frost. But a whole neighborhood valued this one for the link it had to precious people and happy times, to a life that recedes with every death and each passing landmark.

On Monday the charred timbers still smoldered within the sandstone foundation. The red tile silo where Beverly often chalked happy messages to the neighbors—"Welcome Home Jean!" "Yeah, Scott and Kim"—stood blackened and lonely against the sky. But the cats were back, and, said Beverly brightly, "I never realized what a nice view I was missing. Now I can see clear up to Leimbachs!"

Rugby Park

Ah, Rugby in May! Down at the corner Mel Niggle's plum orchard is blooming to beat the band. Cline's creek is running full, and the marsh marigolds line the banks to cheer. Our "boulevards" are fringed with flowers—violets, dandelions, and other spring beauties.

The willows are weeping gold, the pin oaks are unfolding their delicate leaves of red, and the maples drape themselves in lacey seed mantles. The catnip is nipping, the trillium trilling, the bluebells ringing. The jacob's ladder is scaling the riverbanks. The bluebirds are spreading the news that paradise lies just west of the river, north of the hollow, and south of the Ridge.

Garden of Eden—Rugby Corners. When you live in the Garden you should be content. But who ever was? Perhaps all those city folks moving from the suburbs, followed by landscape architects and Chem Lawn men spritzing the crabgrass and the burdock planted the first seeds of discontent.

We grew covetous, and we took on airs. We wanted a park. It didn't take a vote of the town council or the planning commission or even the zoning board. Ninety-six of Rugby's ninety-eight citizens weren't even consulted. There was space available down at the fork, under the End o' Way–Pick-Your-Own sign, where the Schmalzes mow the lawn of the abandoned schoolhouse and Bank Street and Morse Road meet at North Ridge.

Rugby Park is a project planned and executed by the citizenry with no funding whatsoever from the town fathers. You probably wouldn't include it among the great gardens of the Western world—Versailles, Keukenhof, Bellinggrath, Sissinghurst, and the like. It covers only three square feet and boasts nine tulips: six yellow, three red. The foundation planting is a shoot of wild asparagus; the ground cover, a peck of slag.

But last Sunday it was in glorious bloom. Rugby Park was so captivating you stopped seething over the fact that just around the corner somebody had vandalized the 4-H welcome sign or finished off a six-pack and dropped it by the STOP sign.

When you turned off the Ridge and chose a road at the fork, your eye fell on those tulips, and you forgot for a moment that somebody had died who should have lived, that somebody had lived who should mercifully have died, that your fuel bills were up and your oats weren't, that you had a term paper overdue, that your kids had left home and weren't homesick, that you smoked too much and were developing a cough, that May was half over and you hadn't started spring cleaning, that your car payments weren't finished but your car was—everything, you forgot, but that tiny square of beauty. That's all Rugby Park aimed to be, a brief moment in the day when you realized that no matter what else was wrong, living in Rugby was all right.

Two glorious days our park bloomed, and then came the crime. Somebody lopped the heads off our tulips—didn't pick them and take them home to enjoy, just cut off their heads and dropped them there.

A serpent has entered our Eden.

Maggie

Motherhood was the glory of Maggie Kawasaki's life. We knew she had been born in Missouri—carloads of relatives arrived from there each summer—and that she'd been a telephone operator before she married Happy and moved to Brownhelm, where most of her children were born, but that was all. Maggie never talked about herself. I often think she started to die the day her eleventh child left home for good. But between the birth of Edwin (her firstborn) and the departure of Ken (her last), she was totally alive, committed, and content with her lot as mother to eleven and surrogate mother to dozens, my children and me among them.

In that difficult decade following the Depression, people looked with disdain on families having a baby every year or two. A wealthy acquaintance once made the mistake of suggesting to Maggie that perhaps life might be easier for her and Happy if they practiced birth control.

"Why, I wouldn't give the end off one of my babies' fingers for all the money you've got," she snapped. "Things" didn't mean a fig to Maggie, nor did status. People were important for their humanity alone. She and Happy had a brood with varied accomplishments—teachers, engineers, doctors, salesmen, and soldiers among them—and she rejoiced in each achievement, never weighing one above another, extending a little more love and a few more prayers to those who had a harder go of it.

Maggie and Happy and their vacillating tribe—cousins, foster children, and needy friends—lived down on the Ridge at the end of Bank Street in a low and rambling house beneath a sycamore tree. The place was always open, Maggie was always there, and a meal was usually in process. Happy was a chef and brought home number-ten cans of leftovers, which Maggie dispersed like loaves and fishes. It was a wonderfully convenient and congenial place for me to drop my children for an hour or a day or a week or more. I always felt that if I hadn't come back for a year, neither Maggie nor my boys would have noticed.

My father-in-law, who was committed to the German principle of stubborn independence, used to snort about my leaving my boys at Kawasaki's, "like a cowbird laying eggs in somebody else's nest." He didn't understand that Maggie and I for a short and vital time fulfilled each other's needs. Her children were leaving her nest empty, and mine were sometimes too much with me for the ends I was trying to achieve.

My mother-in-law died while Dane was very young, before Teddy and Orrin were born, and it was Maggie who filled the void when there was farm work pressing. All during the potato harvest Maggie would care for the little boys and have a steaming meal ready when we came weary at nightfall to collect them.

Maggie took in stray cats, stray kids, stray relatives, often whole families of strays. No more distinction was ever made between "good" and "bad" people than between black and white, bright and not-so-bright, rich and poor. It was the most egalitarian home imaginable. Anybody with a need could come around to Maggie's house; food, shelter, comfort, and advice were freely given. Maggie grieved a lot, cried a lot, prayed a lot, but never for herself—only for her "kids" and the forlorn souls she took to her heart.

She didn't have "class" as the world assigns it. She enjoyed not wearing either her false teeth or her shoes. She could bellow like a fishwife when the occasion warranted. (Maggie was no pushover where discipline was concerned.) Her house was usually a shambles, but her priorities were never out of order. In her selflessness and her intuitive response to human need, she was almost Christ-like. It was impossible to repay Maggie for the kind of generosity she tendered, but some people tried. My mother-in-law had once given her a slip off a deep purple lilac Maggie had admired.

"I'll plant it out by the road where you can enjoy it as you go by," she told Mrs. Leimbach.

They are both gone these many years but the purple lilac has grown into a handsome tree, and it always serves to remind me what a special blessing I enjoyed in having Maggie Kawasaki as "mother" and friend.

By the Book

The observers of the passing scene in Brownhelm agree unanimously that Patty Miller did all right when she married Chuck Latto. And they 'low as how Chuck did pretty well for himself too. In addition to a sharp gal from one of the "good old families" he got seventy acres of prime farmland on the sandy side south of the Ridge.

Chuck worked his way smoothly into the social structure of Brownhelm by being wisely humble. As a schoolteacher with an unlimited fund of ignorance on rural subjects, Chuck knew better than to rush in and take over like a ninety-day wonder. He puttered around first with a small tract of land, using some old equipment from the forties, drawing a few laughs; raising some corn, an acre of this, and an acre of that. And he sought advice from anyone who would stand still to be interrogated. When George Reinhart, who had rented the bulk of the Miller property since Patty's father died, decided to semiretire, Chuck was ready. Well . . . almost.

He armed himself with a volume of gleanings from *Successful Farming* and the Extension Department's little bible called *Agronomy Guide*. Rumor has it that he was seen walking his fields reading that book.

"He even slept with it under the bed," says Patty.

"I figure I was never more than one chapter ahead of where I needed to be," says Chuck.

Then he did the first thing you do as a greenhorn starting to farm: he went to the Production Credit Association to get his hands on some cash, and he traded in his forties equipment for some of 1962 vintage, a Case Diesel and a four-bottom plow.

He read the "What to Raise" chapter in his bible and decided to go for broke in soybeans. He measured his acreage, diagrammed his fields, and calculated how many bushels of seed he would need. He read up on varieties, consulted all his neighbors, went to a seminar, and then, torn by mental conflict, ordered his seed.

The day Chuck dipped his plow in the ground Patty was there with the camera to record it for posterity. He coupled the hydraulics, aimed the tractor down the row, and roared off, looking back, as the book had described, to check the plow depth.

"Hey! Look out!" shouted Patty, as the front end lifted off the ground and Chuck wheelied down the row. There were uneasy vibrations from the Brownhelm Cemetery across the road as Russell Miller turned over in his grave.

"I should be able to get this thing plowed in a day or two," he mused at the onset. A hundred mishaps later he was not so confident. George Reinhart was shocked when he looked out his window in the middle of one night two weeks later and saw Chuck out there still plowing.

Chuck's fields all lie along the main road into town. He knew he was in for scrutiny from the local pros, and he wasn't taking any chances on a poor stand. He enlisted Patty to follow the planter for the first four acres.

"It's skipping," she hollered.

"I know," he shouted back. "The book says it'll skip from time to time."

"Yes, but ten or twenty feet?" she called. There followed a horrendous clashing of gears, and it was back to the shop to weld a casting.

The day they applied the herbicide Chuck was confounded by the problem of climbing a little rise and losing sight of the row's end. He stationed Patty on the other side of the knoll with a bicycle flag as a target.

"It worked a lot better," said Chuck, "when I discovered I could pivot on the end boom and follow the planter tracks."

Once the crop was in, Chuck began thinking ahead to harvest. *Successful Farming* suggested that "the very small farmer (250 acres) might do well to buy a good used combine."

"Seventy acres isn't even a farm," moaned Chuck. But he found a 1963 machine for $2,300 and spent a couple of weeks going over it with a bucket of grease and ten pounds of welding rod. Anxious to have a trial run, he volunteered to combine Alex More's oats. Alex was delighted. Chuck pulled into the field with all the panache of the Secretary of Agriculture on an $80,000 combine. He had filled one hopper, Patty trotting behind to be certain he was doing a clean job, when all blazes broke loose inside the machine.

"What do you think, Alex?" hollered Chuck.

"Better shut 'er off," said Alex.

Twenty-four hours later—new slip clutch installed—same scene! Chuck combined another forty bushels.

"There's no straw coming out the back," said Patty. There followed more major surgery and a bill for $850. Alex finished his oats with an old Massey Harris Clipper, but Chuck figured he was ready for the soybean harvest.

After church on Sundays Chuck Latto's lush soybeans come in for a lot of comment. Nobody is ready to acknowledge that he owes them to skill or the *Agronomy Guide* or the hovering ghost of Russell Miller.

"Beginner's luck," they josh, but each secretly believes that it was his own input that made the difference. Now Chuck is pumping everybody for advice on when and how to market his beans. But when it comes to making the ultimate mistake for Chuck, they're all hedging.

"I want to go on being your friend," says John Angersbach.

Chuck has read all the chapters on marketing and a lot more stuff on commodities. "Golly," he says. "Isn't it exciting!"

"Chuck," says John, "why don't you throw that blasted book away?"

Just East of West

If you're looking for a place where you won't be overwhelmed by progress, a freeway won't bisect your house, sewer assessments are nil, and the greatest danger your kids may have to face is a stray dog, a rattlesnake, or a very slow freight, you may want to consider Horace, Kansas. Horace lies two miles west of Tribune in Greeley County out by the Colorado border.

Nobody in Tribune, Kansas, will swear that Horace Greeley ever actually set foot in Greeley County. In order to reach the West Coast, he did indeed push through western Kansas, but from the clippings secured under glass in the Historical Museum, it seems clear that he didn't have much good to say about the region. His warmer remarks were reserved for eastern Kansas, which is quite another country from the drylands of western Kansas. "Go West, young man!" either meant go a little farther west, or stop before you get to Greeley County. (Of course, he didn't know it was going to be Greeley County.)

Yet the pioneers of this area clutched at his promise of greatness and memorialized him. The first courthouse was established at Horace, and the neighboring town (the present county seat) was named Tribune in honor of the New York paper of which Greeley was editor.

Horace is not without opportunity, much of it lost and a lot of it faded. The only business flourishing there other than the co-op elevator (which took me there) is the liquor store. The folks from Tribune, which always votes "dry," sneak over to buy their hooch. An entrepreneur might do well with a drive-through carryout store.

Everyone in Greeley County agrees that somebody should reopen Ma Fuller's Café, down next to the railroad and just up the street from the liquor store. "It wasn't a very fancy place, but people came here from miles around. Ma could really put out the food," says Erma John, my hostess in Horace. "Ma ran it for years, and then when she got to be eighty, she just said one day, 'That's it!' She took down the sign and shut the door," and another institution was gone.

Horace approached the point of being a flourishing city at the turn of the century, when the railroad was the lifeblood of the nation. Horace is the division place, where the trains change crews, and the workers sleep over before turning homeward on the next day's shift. In the early days the railroads provided dugouts to house the men. These were in effect deep basements with peaked roofs buried under mounds of sod. At each end was a covered stairway to the surface and an entryway about the size of a privy. They were cool in summer, warm in winter, and, being below ground, an excellent shelter from the persistent wind, the bane of the prairie.

I suppose you could still rent a dugout home in Horace, but you'd have to do a bit of renovating. Most of them are abandoned, and some have caved in altogether. The suggestion that their cool interiors attract rattlesnakes made the notion of living in one less than appealing to me. There is other housing going begging in town. The population's down to 150 or 200, counting rattlers.

Horace isn't exactly the garden spot of Kansas. The Chinese elms struggle to survive the dry winds, as evidenced by the dead wood poking from them. Tumbleweeds blow about the main intersection in town, catching under car bumpers and farm machinery, everywhere forming dirty "petticoats" beneath the shrubbery. Flowers and trees and the meager patches of lawn one sees in western Kansas are wrested from the earth by eternal vigilance. Every morning and evening the gardener must be out there with the hose.

The latest news is that they ran a water line over from Tribune and things are looking up. The YMCA will soon open a dormitory and social hall for the division crews. (Maybe I am wrong in thinking of sewer assessments as no threat.)

The only really fitting word for Horace is "gray." The streets are dusty, the houses have a weather-beaten look, the foliage fights a losing battle. It may not sound terribly desirable, but I keep remembering a little girl from Kansas blown away in a tornado. Though Dorothy was put down in a Technicolor land of infinite wonders, she was obsessed by a solitary wish: to get back to Kansas, a Kansas every bit as forlorn as this little prairie town, perhaps.

Like Dorothy, I find myself yearning to get back to Kansas: Horace, Kansas, an ashen oasis beneath a broad blue sky surrounded by wide fields of wheat in its spring verdure. The April morning I was there three of Erma John's friends came at 7:00 for the daily exercise stint, and we walked a square Kansas mile into those blue-green fields. Like Dorothy, I have learned that the loveliest sights are seen with the heart; it's the people who add the warmth and the color. When I bring to this landscape the friends I made there, well . . . I think Horace Greeley made a grave oversight.

Conservatism—Upper- or Lowercase

When the news came that Margaret Thatcher had been elected Prime Minister of Great Britain, I was down on my knees with my head in the oven. My first impulse was to turn on the gas. But a news photo of me facedown in Easy-Off against a backdrop of brooms, buckets, sweeper hoses, dead spider plants, and bags of sprouted onions would be an ignominy that underscored my failure as a woman in the new age. I swished the old jockey shorts around in the bucket, wrung them out, and went on with the ceremonial rites.

At fifty-three Margaret Thatcher was head of a great nation. At fifty-one I didn't even qualify as head of a household. Yet Margaret and I started out on something of a par. Her father was a grocer, and my mother ran a farm market. In my only bid for office, however, I was defeated by a single vote (for class secretary in 1944). It was not a crippling defeat, really: if I had voted for myself, I would have won. Then what went wrong? Why was she breathing the rarefied air of No. 10 Downing Street while I was suffocating on ammonia fumes?

Margaret Thatcher was a winner because she is a Conservative. I too am a conservative. It's all this conserving that has undone me. I am totally bogged down in conservatism and its routines. In a house with four beds, for example, I have twenty-one blankets (most of which no self-respecting swami would wrap around himself). The logistics of that projected through nine rooms to include the possessions of five people, their conditioning strongly influenced by my own, over twenty-eight years—the shifting, sifting, sorting, mending, handling, harboring, cleaning, painting required of all that stuff —well, it boggles the mind.

Conservatism mandates a way of life that gives me pause where Margaret Thatcher is concerned. The practical difference between Conservatives and Liberals is the difference between being bound and being free, between earning the bread and giving it away.

And so I wondered, as I pushed on through my household routines, Who makes the bread at Margaret Thatcher's house? Who freezes the spinach and pickles the beets? Who fits the pockets into Denis' trousers? Who tears the sheets down the middle and sews the selvages together? Who checks the *Manchester Guardian* for the weekly food buys? Who folds and files the grocery bags? Who stokes the furnace?

What would the Prime Minister do when confronted, at the bottom

21

of a junk drawer, with a mess of bolts and brads and bits of wire, razor blades and rubber bands, marbles and flashlight batteries, all mixed in with strands of steel wool and fiberglass and mouse droppings? Would she give it a liberal toss into the trash? Or conservatively pick through, sort, file, and discard?

The future of Great Britain could hang in the balance.

Eye of the Beholder

"In her letters and her essays Flannery O'Connor reports the activities of her peacocks with the dull eye of a farm wife," writes a critic in *Saturday Review*.

You can imagine that the eye of this farm wife, falling on that appraisal, gleamed with sudden fire. Perhaps it was an idle metaphor thoughtlessly dropped; nonetheless, it had the earmarks of a Freudian slip. Who, I wondered, was the prototype of this dull-eyed farm wife in the narrow mind of this reviewer? Some peasant heroine from Dostoevski? Flaubert? Hardy? Stendahl? She surely didn't get it on location in America.

I've met thousands of farm wives, and I can't think of a single one I would classify thus. Each of them seems convinced that providence has set her down in a singular Eden. A farm wife watching the same piece of property in all its rounds, year after year, perceives wonders invisible to the less committed. And she has a peculiar capacity for seeing beyond the ugly and the commonplace to the promising and the rare.

Every day my mailman brings me letters from farm women. Often they thank me for expressing a thought they couldn't articulate; they often proceed then to express other things in ways that make me envious.

"Your book has released a flood of memories—the smell of onions, Polish sausage, and potatoes fixed by the panful to feed the hobos during Depression years; the Mexican boy who sang under my window, loading market trucks at 2:00 a.m., the metal wheels and the cleats on my penny loafers clicking on the storage floor, the soft Southern voices of the drivers. . . . Stop by someday so I can show you how lovable a cow can be." That farm woman had a keen nose and a keen ear to go with her keen eye.

A Montana farm woman wrote, "Once you've lived under these wide skies, you can't go back East— Oh, no."

From an Idaho wife: "I have chased an autumn sunset across the Kansas plains and into the dusk of Colorado. . . . A sunrise bouncing its gorgeous hues off the snowfields of the Sawtooth range last Christmas morning provided a surprise Christmas gift. The majesty of Wyoming plains never fails to thrill me. The wheatlands of Kansas, Colorado, Idaho, waving their golden heads in perpetual sweeps—if one hasn't seen this, has one lived?"

From the Red River Valley, a picture of the urgency of farm life: "Sugar beet harvest! It's amazing how the Valley comes to life for a last gasp before winter, all night long and all during the day. I made a run to town for parts at midnight (they're open 24 hours), and everywhere I looked were lights—farmers combining, fertilizing, plowing."

A bit of philosophy came from another: "I have the explorer in me somewhere, and it surfaces in these jaunts alone. . . . There is a value in companionship, but solitude has its own special reward."

A farm wife in Illinois (who is printing her own illustrated book on a handpress) shares a spot of beauty: "Stuck a twig of lilac in a Kickapoo Indian bottle on the windowsill. BEEUTIFUL!"

From the Connecticut Valley: " . . . a glorious countryside of brown-velvet earth shooting green onion blades and emerald spears of young corn shoots—all worked by the Polish women with their heads wrapped in bandanas."

"Dull eye" indeed!

Refrigerator Trauma

Back in the fifties we had a high school girl working for us whose mother compelled her to stay home every Thursday night of her life and clean the refrigerator. If she has not by now freed herself of that enslavement, I calculate that by the time she's eighty, she will have spent five working years of her life bathing cold coils and poking about in musty hydrators! By the same reckoning I will have invested only two weeks.

Once every eight months or so doesn't seem too often to clean a refrigerator. I would let it go longer, I suppose, but my husband is only tolerant to a point, and I know he has passed that point when I come downstairs of a morning to find the refrigerator "disemboweled": the contents strewn like viscera across the sink, the stove, the table, and the countertop.

"If you'd sell the penicillin rights to that refrigerator, we could probably put the kids through college," says Paul, fighting his way to the sink through a reeking mass of leaking lettuce bags, sweating pickle jars, chunks of petrified cheese, and malodorous morsels of spoiled meat wrapped in wrinkled aluminum foil. "Now why in the world would anyone harbor two pints of sour cream that has aged to gray cheese?"

"Don't touch that! I'm gonna take it back to Safeway. It was already spoiled when I got it for Easter."

"In three weeks' time it looks like that?"

"Not this Easter, LAST Easter. I keep forgetting to return it."

"I give up!" mutters Paul.

"What I can't figure out is why we're keeping that little jar of water in the door shelf. I think it's been in there for three years," says Orrin.

"Oh, that's a leftover drink. I keep thinking that someday a bonafide drinker will wander through here, and then when one does, I forget to serve it."

"Why don't you use it to reconstitute those two dried olives?" he says, indicating a tall, thin, lidless bottle from which two shriveled olives stare like bloodshot eyes.

"Very funny," I mutter, fishing a slimy cucumber out of the hydrator.

"Does any family really need seven mason jars of french fry grease?" asks Paul.

"That's what I was wondering," I say. "Then when I dumped them together, I discovered that one was a quart of iced tea and two were mulled cider left over from New Year's. That darker jar is syrup for making cinnamon apples."

"And the last time we had cinnamon apples was Thanksgiving. . . . Right?"

"Well, it'll be around again in only six months," I say weakly.

"What's this stuff?" he asks, unscrewing the lid from a jar of reddish liquid. "Smells like hooch."

"That's a kind of oriental wine Helen gave me to make her Chinese chicken dish."

"For crying out loud! Helen's been dead for five years!"

24

"I know, that's the trouble. I've lost the recipe."

"You know, dear, your sister's got that terrific thing she does with leftovers. Why don't you try it?"

"What's that?"

"She throws them out!"

Annual Hoedown

It struck me as a dreary little country high school gymnasium, but then, I wasn't there when it was still the showplace of the county, the night they beat McClure for the county championship and rang the school bell with such fervor that they turned it over in its yoke. I wasn't part of the quartet who won the talent show here in 1950 with a rolling rendition of "Rag Mop," nor did I tearfully cross that stage to a labored "Pomp and Circumstance." This place did not echo with the strains of my own puberty rites.

The crowd was a little thin for the annual alumni banquet this spring.

"Where is everybody?" asked the president.

"Costs too much," grumbled a few people who wanted their opinions expressed anonymously.

"Speak up. We can't hear you," said the president.

"If you want my opinion," said the center forward of the 1939 girls' basketball team, "I don't think we need a paid speaker."

"We got plenty of talent right here among our graduates," says the center guard of the 1939 girls' basketball team, who is sitting next to her. There were affirmative mumbles from scattered members of the audience.

"What about the band? Did you all like the Valley Five, the one we had last year? Let me see a show of hands if you liked them," said the president, dealing loosely with Robert's Rules and attempting to shift the dissidents from the embarrassing subject of the "paid speaker."

"Yeah, but they was only the Valley Three last year," quipped another dissident.

"Mr. President," said the orator of the class of '41, rising heavily to his feet. "Mr. President, I'd like to know if you paid those three musicians all of the fee agreed upon for five musicians."

"Yes, Lawrence, I did."

"Well, Mr. President, it doesn't seem right to me that three men should be paid the same as five when it was five that was agreed upon. What I mean is, if only three play instead of five, they ought to earn three-fifths of what was agreed upon, if you see what I mean."

"Everybody danced and enjoyed the music and had a good time, so I paid them what they asked." Around the room there were disturbed mutterings about this attack on the president. "If you want to make these arrangements next year, Lawrence, that's just fine with me. I only took the job because nobody else would take it. The floor is now open for nominations for next year's president."

Somebody was nominated, and somebody else (who hadn't won an "A" in parliamentary procedure) seconded the nomination. Somebody moved that the nominations cease, and next year's sacrificial lamb was elected by unanimous ballot. In a similar process of railroading, the whole slate was elected, and the subject of the $25-a-couple fee broke out again, as a fire will do that has not been completely suppressed.

"For years now some of us have been paying the bills out of our own pockets. Last year, if you remember, we passed the hat to pay the bills, and I made up my mind that I wasn't going to do that again," said the retiring president. "Now if you take your wife and go into Toledo, have a nice dinner with a beverage in a place where you can dance, you sure ain't gonna do it for less than $25—and you don't get a paid speaker!"

But, of course, this wasn't Toledo, and they weren't having any drinks, and the lights were bright enough that you could read the watermark on the mimeographed programs. This was old Malinta High, and even a professional caterer slicing rare beef on a chopping block didn't banish the specter of the Band Mothers hovering about. For $25 they ought to be entitled to a few crepe paper streamers, a wishing well, Syracuse china, and Dr. Joyce Brothers.

When the dust finally settled, the new seniors—already well indoctrinated—were welcomed, the anniversary classes were heard from, the glory of old Malinta High was raised in song and story, and the "paid speaker" was finally introduced.

She told them, first off, that she agreed with them, that they didn't need a paid speaker, for which she received applause. Then she went on to reinforce her opinion by telling them what they already knew well: what it is to be pupil, teacher, parent, and alumnus of a little country high school.

26

She collected her share of the $25 fees and made her way toward the exit as two members of the Valley Five came struggling in with an amplifier and a couple of guitar cases. "I hope you've got three more guys out there in the van," she said.

Litany for a Church Luncheon

Thou knowest, Lord, that this is the day of the big church luncheon for the garden club, and that I am in charge. I will have much need of Thee today. Be with me.

It's never been really clear to me, Lord, how you felt about church dinners, whether when You said, "Feed My sheep," You had garden club ladies in mind. Sometimes I think not. But it's too late to fret about that, Lord. They're all counting on us, You and me (and ladies who tend gardens are more aware of your miracles than the common herd).

I have done what I could, Lord, to make this day run smoothly, but there are little ways in which You could be of service. Let the count be nigh unto that which the chairman gave so there is sufficient beef to spread over the rice, and let not there be a mountain of rice left when the ladies have distributed their door prizes and gone.

Would You see that all the gelatins mold firmly, Lord, so that when turned out on lettuce leaves, they run not like soup about the plate?

Inspire those women of the pie committee, Lord, that they not prepare their "homemade" pies from boxes, but from the fruits of their own labors.

Forgive my reserving Alida's chocolate angel pie for the kitchen crew, for verily she is the best cook in the parish.

Keep tempers cool in our hot kitchen, Lord; Thou knowest that each woman is mistress of her own kitchen but that church kitchens suffer from a surplus of bosses, each doing things her way.

Be watchful over the fuses, Lord, that the beverage chairman not discover when the last plate has been served that the coffee is yet unbrewed.

Deliver us from the spilling of coffee or any other thing upon these garden ladies, each decked out like a lily of the field. Lay a mantle of patience upon them, making them mindful that even next week it may be they who serve the Rotarians down at the church kitchen.

But please, Lord, smite the club president ere she crieth, "Would the cooks come out of the kitchen and take a bow?"

Grant that there may be a little profit and that when the committee meet to haggle over its disbursement, we may remember Thee and Thy goodness, deciding not in favor of bigger, brighter kettles for more and better suppers but remembering, rather, that there are those with empty bowls to whom leftover rice is inconceivable. Amen.

Auction Appraisal

Auction Saturday at Brownhelm Center: The widow Arndt went on to her reward last year, and the executrix was settling her affairs.

A bright sun blessed the day, and Gwendolyn Arndt's worldly goods were set on the lawn in orderly rows at right angles to the neat little house where she had lived out her days, three doors down from Brownhelm School. In a prominent place out front were the smaller furniture items—dressers, mirrors, end tables, chairs. The ladies of the E & R Church held forth in the garage with coffee and doughnuts, hot dogs and homemade pie.

A goodly crowd milled about the yard, filed through the house, and peered into the shed out back, appraising the boxes, baskets, and crates of assorted goods, the tools and machinery, the lumber and the property itself. Those who had made the tour of the grounds stood about with their hands in their pockets, chatting about the possibilities with neighbors or strangers or friends of last week's auction. (A sizable portion of any auction crowd consists of regulars, people whose vocation or avocation it is to acquire used goods.) Everybody's friendly auctioneer, Jim Wagner, was there with his cane and his portable sound system.

"What can we sell you today?" he said, thrusting his glad hand forward in a hearty shake.

"Not a thing," I said. "For every piece of junk here, I've got ten at home."

"It's all in the point of view," he said, moving to get the action under way.

My friends Long-Shot Larry and Horse-Trader Harry were there. They had already sized up the collection. "Not much here," said

Larry. "There's an oak Victrola in good condition that'll bring good money, and an icebox down in the cellar I'd like to have. It'll probably go for four or five hundred."

Standing near the china and the linens was a friend from my grade school years. "What brings you here?" I asked.

"I used to work with Mrs. Arndt. Nice lady. Lotta fun."

I moved about the yard, making my own appraisals. An oak dresser with an oval mirror stirred warm vibrations. It could have been the one in which my parents kept their meager things, though this was better preserved.

I wandered then through the house with the rest of the curious, examining the larger furniture items, wondering why. It seemed a monstrous act to gaze impersonally on these relics of an unknown life, coveting or dismissing them as worthless for one's own purposes. It was a sad and dreary collection of pieces, mostly late Roosevelt, early Eisenhower, naked now without the antimacassars, doilies, pictures, and bric-a-brac that had given them personality and marked them as valued possessions of the Widow Arndt. And the appurtenances strewn on tables out back or heaped pell-mell into grocery carts to be pawed through by unfeeling strangers were similarly profaned.

Here was a box of old greeting cards—valentines with cherubs and paper lace, postcards from once fashionable resorts long gone, photographs of familiar landmarks in unfamiliar virgin state, baptismal certificates and Sunday school attendance awards—the fallen leaves of a once verdant life. Other boxes contained yellowed, handworked pillowcases, dresser scarves and table runners of percale and linen with intricate edgings of tatting or crochet, frugally preserved—hope chest items, all, whose hope went unfulfilled while the widow made do with worn muslin. The whole thing was out of joint.

I moved through the back door and inched to the front of the crowd that was following the sale. "Who'll give a dollar? . . . Now two? . . . Now three? . . ." They were selling the garden tools. My eye fell on a coal shovel grouped with a rake, a spade, and a couple of hoes. I could use that coal shovel, but it was too late. "Sold! for five dollars."

I left then to go home and cook lunch for Paul, returning at 1:30. The crowd had thinned to the earnest buyers of the important pieces. Harry was leaving with assorted items in the back of his truck, a "coal oil" heater among them. Larry had a checklist of what he'd bought and what he'd resold to other buyers. John Love was wandering out of the house.

"What'd you buy, John?"

"Two hot dogs," he said.

The yard was empty now save for the litter of paper cups and cigarette wrappers. I saw the man who had bought the shovels and the garden tools moving off with them. I called to him.

"Did you really want that coal shovel? I'll give you three bucks for it."

"You can have it for four."

I peeled four dollars from the wad in my pocket and took possession.

The crowd moved indoors for what were deemed the most desirable items. The cherry dining room set went for $450, the Victrola with all the records for $200 to a girl who squealed and clapped her hands. Larry bought the icebox for less than he was prepared to pay. He started to collect the cartons of sundry stuff he'd acquired, a portable wringer among them.

"What are you going to do with all that junk, Larry?"

"I'm saving it for my garage sale," he laughed.

"See you all next Saturday over at Amherst," said the auctioneer.

I picked up the coal shovel and went home.

It was too big for my furnace door.

Summer

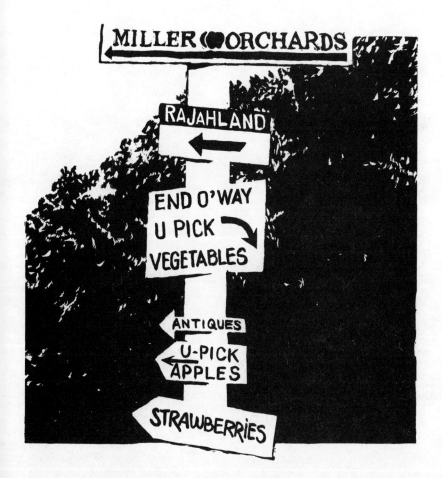

*I want to capture summer
In the middle of a dawn,
Press it fast between two pages now,
Before the magic's gone.*

—Eileen Black, "August"

Port of Call

My sister and her husband have sold "the Menz place," and the thought brings a lump to my throat. It isn't just any house in a parade of moves and removals. It was built by one of the old families in town in the heyday of the Victorian era. It occupies the choicest, most generous homesite that our town affords—two minutes from school and five minutes from the square, within earshot of the fire siren and the Congregational church bell, yet surprisingly isolated by a wooded gorge to the east and the village cemetery on the north.

It stands on a hill high above Main Street. Two sprawling Muego pines stand sentinel to the broad stone steps descending the terraced yard, steps used now only by the mailman and the paperboy. It was designed with the features of a time that could afford to be lavish—ten sizable rooms, front and back stairways, a pantry, a dumbwaiter, a spacious attic, a parlor opened for holidays and weddings or properly secluded for the laying out of the dear departed.

It also had antiquated plumbing, skimpy closets, a woeful kitchen, and water draining to the sewer through the basement. From the day the Kovaches took it over from the Menzes, they were constantly adapting it to the needs of their family of eight.

They began with moving the sink across the kitchen and ended by

33

remodeling everything. They moved a stairway, reshaped the porches, and added two baths, a guest house, and a covered patio large enough to shelter half the town from a Fourth of July deluge. Gone now is the down-at-the-heels look that characterized much of the twenty-seven years of transition. (I used to stop by and plant a few petunias by the lamppost so that no one would think it abandoned.) Gone too are the children who grew up happily here in well-ordered comfort. The energies once expended on them have been trained on the house and the grounds in recent years.

In its latest metamorphosis, "the Menz place" is perhaps more sophisticated than its architects of change. Where once a dozen cousins dug in a sandpile beneath the maple, now a spotlight illumines green lawn and night branches. Bay windows look out on yards of ornamental shrubs and manicured borders. A Japanese garden next to the drive adds a touch of the exotic.

All the fixing and the changing and the remodeling have been accomplished. Everything is as Mary and Frank dreamed of it twenty-seven years ago—just what they thought a family of eight could enjoy, and more. But now the requirements are different. A couple facing retirement alone don't need ten rooms, two verandas, a guest house, and grounds calling for a gardener.

A home is not owned just by the folks who pay the taxes. It is the wider possession of those who have loved it for whatever reason, those who have regaled themselves at its galas, groaned at its Thanksgiving boards, or found heart's ease around its kitchen table. I am one of those. The big house on South Main with its convenience, its familiarity, its comfort, and its love was the closest thing I had to a second home. And my needs have not changed with respect to this house.

It was never locked, and nearly everytime I was in town I stopped by on some mission—to use the phone or the bathroom or the sewing machine, to make myself a cup of coffee or a bit of lunch, to do my ironing on the Kovach mangle or my washing with their city water in a season of drought. I often dropped my children here or picked up a cousin or two to take home. Paul and I sat in this kitchen with Frank and Mary and timed my labor pains when Ted was born.

Once I spent a week as "writer in residence" revising a book, sitting at the glass table on the screened-in porch secluded by a dense growth of Dutchman's pipe.

Always when I happened in, I read the letters from the children grown and gone, studied the notes around the kitchen that kept me alert to the currents of the house, then left one of my own: "I was here, but you weren't. So-and-so called, told them you'd call back. Borrowed your chafing dish. Thanks."

The children have come home and shed their tears, accepted the practical reality of a move their hearts will never make. They have sorted through the bags labeled "Sylvia," "Michael," "Karen," "Chris," "Stephanie," and "Brett" and decided who wants what of the things the folks won't have room for in a smaller home.

I am waiting patiently for word of which one of them wants Aunt Pat.

Blarney from the Light-foot Lads

On the first Saturday after the last soybeans are planted, and a week or two before the wheat is ripe, a few thousand brawny, sun-tanned farm lads will lead to the altar, like lambs to sacrifice, a corresponding number of rose-lipt maidens. Each of these girls will have gone the bridal shower route. She will come luxuriously dowered by friends and family with crockpots, electric blankets, broiler ovens, chafing dishes, pillowcases embroidered with her initial, towel sets in "her" colors, china in "her" pattern, and lingerie to match her eyes.

The happy everafter is about to begin in a shiny new mobile home or in the former tenant house on the other place, smelling of fresh paint and new wallpaper, greening with spider plants and Swedish ivy. This girl has just about everything a girl could want—and nothing she really needs!

She thinks of this as a marriage, little realizing it is in effect an incorporation. She sees herself as "wife," dangerously innocent of cosigner, bookkeeper, truck driver, "go-fer," herdsman, labor boss, and general farmhand.

If I could send her a shower gift, it would be a few nickels' worth of advice. I would forewarn her that a farmer is a notorious practitioner of the double entendre. Oh, he'll tell her that he's plainspoken, says what he means. Even he is oblivious of the subliminal implications of much of his "farmspeak" . . . :

"As long as you're going to town, stop by the hardware and bring me home a roll of binder twine" means, forget the shopping trip. He needs the binder twine p.d.q.

"You bake a better pie than my mother" simply means, his mother wasn't much of a cook.

"I see where J. B. Huge is selling out on Saturday" says clearly, "No, I'm not going over and help insulate the parsonage Saturday."

"Somebody's got to go to the mill today" must be understood as, "Pack up the kids and your knitting. The truck's out front with the motor going."

"I bought a real jewel at J. B.'s sale" warns you well in advance that he's planning to spend the winter restoring an old Farmall M.

"I notice Bev Schmalz is out disking" means, "What are you doing around the house here that's so all-fired important?"

"I'd rather have you handling the machinery than anybody I could hire" translates as, "I can't afford to hire anybody to operate the machinery."

"If that sow farrows, I'll be going to the banquet late" should say to you, "Take the kids and go alone."

"I think the car will make it another year or two" is his subtle way of saying, "I just ordered a pickup truck."

"Have you got a minute you can spare?" warns you to pack a lunch, put on your old clothes, and wear your boots and work gloves.

"Jeez! It's hot in this kitchen!" implies, "I've had a long, grueling day in the air-conditioned cab of my combine."

"Did that guy call about coming to do some tiling for us?" is an easy letdown for, "We're not taking that Hawaiian tour this year either."

"Do you ever miss your old job and think about going back to work?" shouldn't fool any farm wife. It means, "I've got a chance to buy a good piece of land."

. . . Ah well, she'll learn, intuitively, as we all do. It's possible that once upon a moonlight evening, he said, "Smell that wild blackberry in bloom, would you!" and she heard him saying, "I had more reasons for becoming a farmer than just getting rich." If she read that one right, she'll be okay.

Ol' Man River

I was almost fifty before I saw the Mississippi River. I had already seen the Rhine, the Rhône, the Seine, the Thames, the Danube, and all the great rivers of the eastern United States. But this was THE river, the epitome of flowing waters, the adventure before which those on all other rivers dimmed.

It was a gentle June day with clean skies and long clear views as I gradually descended the western banks from Iowa. (I had crossed westward in the darkness the previous night.) This day had been planned like a lover's tryst—arrive before noon, assemble a picnic, find a captivating spot, and pass an idle hour in communion.

I cut toward the river from the main highway and found a scrappy little cottage town, where I bought provisions in a bait store. Then I drove along the banks until I found my spot, not one of those "scenic views" with picnic table, refuse can, and safe drinking water, but a deserted dock of rough planks silvering in the sun, reached by an unsteady set of decaying steps. I climbed down, spread my "feast," and discovered the Mississippi.

One of life's rare and perfect hours it was, all the elements fitting together as anticipated: the rediscovery of summer warmth in the mild air, the distant droning of an outboard, the mingling smells of motorboat and fish, the lap . . . lap . . . lap of the ripples beneath the dock, the Coca Cola and the bologna sandwiches (no place, certainly, for wine and cheese)—simple sensual pleasures devoid of philosophy.

I wasn't prompted that morning to wonder why I was so intrigued by the Mississippi, why I had been drawn to keep this appointment. There were no mountain peaks or castle ruins, no sirens on shoals, no storied swans or scholars crewing, no chateaux or towered bridges. Just a very broad, muddy river with several barges passing, forested bluffs in the distance, and a few stationary fishermen.

It wasn't until several years later, when I had occasion to visit Hannibal, Missouri, that I thought again about that day and managed to identify the peculiar charm of the Mississippi. Surely it has figured powerfully in the history, the commerce, the prosperity of the nation, but before we were concerned with history or commerce we knew the Mississippi as the water wonderland of Tom Sawyer and Huckleberry Finn.

Before our brains were crisscrossed by Magellan and Balboa, secants and sectors, light waves and laser beams, we had charted the alleys of Hannibal, the footpaths to the cave, and the pushing-off place to Johnson's Island—the unforgettable territory of the eternal summer of our youth.

There is something stirring, exciting even, in walking down Hill Street in Hannibal, Missouri, coming upon the narrow, green-shuttered Twain house, and thinking, "There! .That's where he really lived, the boy who was Tom Sawyer." To twist the old knobs and enter the tiny rooms furnished with the spare severe pieces of a century ago is to yearn for a lost simplicity. The dreams of life lived in these rooms were not dwarfed by its trappings.

One of the great sorrows of childhood for bookish little creatures like myself was surrendering those captivating landscapes of make-believe to the drabness of reality. What a satisfying paradox forty years later to walk those streets, ponder that river, and recognize that in some few, remarkable places the make-believe and the real intermingle.

Actions Speak Louder

I came steaming up the road at 11:00 one June night following two weeks of self-imposed exile to work solitarily at a writing project, humming, "Gee, it's good to be back home again," pushing my foot a little harder on the accelerator as I came closer and the road became more familiar.

Will somebody be home? Will the lawn be mowed? Will the house be clean? Wonder if the raspberries are ripe?

Question piled on question as the shapes of home materialized. The lights are on; they must be here. The grass is mowed! Here come my dogs, tails wagging, tongues licking.

I knew from experience that nobody would rush out to meet me and carry my bags. ("She liberated herself. Let her carry her own stuff.") There are no outstretched arms, no effusive hellos, how-are-you's, or how'd-it-go's. That is not the cool Germanic way.

"Well, look who's home," said Ted, as I opened the door and took note of the sweeper tracks across the carpet. They were all watching the 11:00 news. Nobody stirred.

"Flip on the garage light," he said, as I fumbled at the switches.

Wow! They'd cleaned the garage. Slick as a whistle. And . . . will you look at that! New storage cupboards! Eight years I've been nagging for those cupboards! A whole wall of new plywood, shiny hinges, latches. I don't believe this!

"Flip on the porch light," Ted said, while I was still reeling from the shock of the garage.

Gollee! They painted the porch floor, laid the rattan rugs, got out the furniture, and . . . Holy cow! A new aluminum ceiling! The light fixtures have new red paint. There's even a bouquet of calendulas on the table. All ready for a summer party!

By now they were on their feet and grinning broadly, coming out to catch my full reaction, filling me in on the complications of these extensive improvements.

"Ted sat on his duff and watched me and Dad work," said Orrin.

"Every good job needs a boss," said Ted.

"How do you like that porch color?" said Orrin. "We put muriatic acid on it and everything."

"Good thing you're home," said Ted. "Cherries need picking."

They rattled on till bedtime with the incidental details of life in my absence. Then we turned out the lights, and Paul and I settled down to the sort of pillow talk that a farmer and his wife share after thirty years of running a farm together:

"How many baskets of beans have you picked?"

"Fifty, Monday; seventy-five, Tuesday. Terribly dry. Been over all the potatoes once with the irrigation, start again next week if we don't get rain."

"How's the wheat?"

"Looks good. Not quite ready yet."

"How about the soybeans?"

"Good. Got a good weed kill. Hoed the melons last week. Sold some soybeans at $6.22. Jumped 80 cents next three days."

"Have plenty of help?"

"Yup. Peter's on vacation. Everybody else's been here. Had twenty-nine or thirty kids."

"What's the price of green beans?"

"They're going for $3.75. Watered them yesterday. Should have a good picking Saturday."

"Raspberries ready?"

"Put ten quarts in the freezer last week. . . ."

Nobody has to tell me they're glad to see me.

I don't have to say that I'm glad to be home.

Six-Thirty Love

The work ethic dies slowly in me. I seldom devote more than an hour of an average day to leisure. I dream of a mythical tomorrow when I shall sit in a chintz-covered chair by a morning window reading *War and Peace*, but something tells me crabgrass or the Gray Panthers will interfere. The dream alone is enough to give me guilt pangs. A farm wife stands in a productive tradition, and certain things are forbidden, like an afternoon of golf or a morning of bridge.

But what about tennis before breakfast?

Nonsense! You don't drive fifteen miles round trip to town to get a little exercise, however exhilarating the notion, not just any old day of the week.

But what if you have to go to town anyway?

Well . . . if it doesn't interfere with anything else to which you're committed, maybe that would be forgiven. . . . And so it is that I tiptoe out at 6:30 on summer days to keep a tennis date with my friend Molly.

Early morning is still the best-kept secret around. Mist envelops the valley; sunlight streams between the trees in shafts so distinct that God could descend upon them. The rabbits and birds have a clear understanding that the world is theirs alone. A spiderweb glistens on the spirea bush next to the corncrib.

I back the pickup out of the barn with no fear of running down a hired boy or a bean customer and tool down the corridor that is Bank Street when Schmalz's corn is as high as an elephant's eye. I often cover the seven and a half miles to town without seeing another car, and if I hesitate and move through the red stoplights, there's nobody to say me nay.

Molly is always at the courts before me. She rides over on her bicycle, bringing a broom to sweep the court if there's been any rain. We greet and exchange comments on the day or what has transpired since yesterday, then we play tennis. It's not Evert-Lloyd and Navratilova, but it's great recreation.

Our tennis is better than our scoring, so we've evolved an abacus of sorts: we have collected a pile of cherry pits at net center, and whoever wins a game gets a cherry pit in her court. We seldom have time for more than one set, but we get in a handful of good volleys and a few solid zings.

Then it's 7:42. We zip the covers on our rackets and bid a quick goodbye. Or if it's a kind of day when we've worked up a real sweat, we quit early, go around the corner to Molly's house, and take a hasty plunge in her pool. Then I pull on my clothes, hop in the pickup, and tear for the town hall, where twenty or thirty blue-jeaned kids are languishing about the bandstand.

They pile in the truck, and at 7:45 on the button we head for the farm. At 7:58 we reenter the corn corridor and arrive at End o' Way, now swarming with kids and cars, tractors and pick-your-own-corn customers. Paul and the boys have loaded a wagon with bundles of baskets, and I drop my precious cargo where they are assigning rows in the bean field.

I take the corn customers in hand, and the day begins. All I missed was breakfast.

Fruit of the Bush

Browsing in one of those artsy-craftsy gift shops in Jackson Hole, Wyoming, one spring I came across a ceramic tea tile decorated with a cluster of green beans hanging from a leafy stalk. Paul would find fault with its botany, I knew—it was crafted with more of an eye for aesthetics than authenticity—but I bought it anyway. It's a satisfying reminder that somebody sees extraordinary beauty in the common stuff of our everyday life.

One by one our bean fields have worn themselves away with the summer. There were five of them, planted at two-week intervals from late April through early June, a new planting going in as the previous emerged.

A good field of green beans will stand as high as two feet and completely fill the space between rows at the onset of the picking. Small wonder that Paul trembles on the morning we take our army of thirty to fifty kids up to tackle them for the first go-around. The hope is that when the sun is high and they all crowd on the wagon to ride back to the barn with the morning's harvest of beans, the vines will still be standing for a second or third picking.

But lush bean vines are tender prey for a carefree kid of twelve with short legs and an aching back who was enticed to this folly by the boy next door flashing five or ten bucks around the neighborhood last payday. Four hours and seven baskets later, when he's been coaxed and nagged and bullied a hundred and fifty yards up the row, he feels pretty good about himself and his morning's work. His head is aswim with addition and multiplication and payday projections. The fact that the bean row in his wake looks as if it had been chewed by a beaver doesn't trouble him much.

It's my poor husband who suffers. Paul has devoted more than forty years of his life to the cultivation of good green beans. That morning's stand of tall, leafy bushes was a horticultural triumph. For all his fears, however, the bean plants usually revive and produce with surprising abundance.

Paul is fussy about his beans. He wants them young and straight and tender, vivid green and disease-free. Once the bean seeds begin to form in the fleshy interior, he's ready to move to the next field.

Putting a good product on the market involves more than just producing it. You have to get it into the basket and off to market in prime condition, and you can't accomplish that by sending a flock of kids up in the field and turning them loose. So despite the management articles saying a manager can't afford to work in the fields, Paul keeps his back bent over his bean rows, supervising and encouraging his band of little bean pickers, and picking enough beans in his lifetime to feed a few million people.

Hand-picked beans are fast becoming the exclusive luxury of the backyard gardener. We're on our last generation of bean pickers here; they come in smaller numbers and with more reluctance. The minimum wage sounded the death knell. They can find easier work at the hourly wage.

Perhaps we'll replace them with a mechanical harvester, as Western growers have had to replace the migrant. It's the only cost-effective way to beat the cheap-food system. But I don't want to be there the first morning that harvester chews its way down those knee-high rows, spewing the bean fodder to the rear. I think I shall miss the little bean stompers.

A bearded fellow graying at the temples drove up recently in a deluxe van, got out with a wife and three daughters, and approached me, saying, "You probably won't remember me, but . . ." Who could have forgotten Roger Benner? I had a flashback to a long-ago bean field where a sandy-haired kid with freckles struggled down the row with two sixteen-pound baskets of beans, his little sister behind him, even more overladen. Roger's baskets were always overfull, he never missed a day of bean picking, and he was always the first to volunteer for overtime hoeing, lawn mowing, market-going—anything. It was

no surprise to find that he now administers a large school system up
in Michigan.

They show up often, these responsible young men and women
saying, "Maybe you don't remember me, but I'll never forget *you*.
You taught me how to work!"

The metaphors of fruition are heavily weighted to grapes hanging
low in shaded arbors or to corn growing golden in withered husks. At
End o' Way, however, a cluster of long, straight green beans hanging
among heart-shaped leaves says it all.

Hang Your Clothes on a Hickory Limb

Orrin just buzzed down the road on his motorcycle, a large tractor
inner tube slung round his shoulder. The picking kids are on lunch
break and are having a free-for-all in the farm pond, refreshing sport
following four ninety-degree hours in the bean fields. Last guy in's a
rotten egg!

Summer was a succession of swimming holes when I was a kid.
The earliest was a wide place in the creek fringed with willow and
wild iris, where bottle flies circled and bull frogs abounded. Depth
ranged normally from six inches to three feet, and the bottom was
gumbo. There was a granite boulder from which we launched our
"belly whoppers" or performed the classic "ham n' eggs." (Hold your
nose and jump, in sitting position.)

The only time the creek was deep enough for "serious swimmin' "
was immediately following a gully washer, and quick as the storm
subsided we snatched our sun-bleached suits from the line and
dashed for the pasture.

There was a secret clearing in the thorn apples where we changed
our clothes. "Bathhouse" was not part of the vocabulary, nor was
toilet. When you felt the urge you merely scampered off deeper into
the thorn apples.

I learned to swim in that mud hole at "high tide," and the moment
when first my feet floated free from the bottom stands out as a mile-
stone in childhood. Even today the sight of a pasture creek at flood
stage stirs barefoot yearnings within.

Neighboring our farm was a spacious park cemetery, with large
lagoons fed by our creek where it had been dammed at the property

line. As soon as we could swim, outgrowing the pasture mud, we appropriated the rear lagoon as our swimming hole. The bottom was just as gooey, but when you could swim, the bottom was irrelevant. We centered our swimming around a couple of big rocks that lay just beneath the water's surface. (Plymouth Rock and Devil's Island, we called them.)

Mr. Yaeger, the cemetery proprietor, spiffed up in tie and French-cuffed shirt, came around in his big blue Buick and evicted us from time to time, but with dogged regularity we crept back, and eventually he left us alone.

"Mr. McGregor"—as we called him—finally accepted what many another concerned property owner has learned about swimming holes, that anarchy is the beauty of the place. (We have three irrigation ponds and a deep hole in the river where kids come to swim. Paul chases out the strangers among them, but they're persistent as dandelions.)

Kids delight in a place where no rules are posted: "Take showers . . . wear bathing caps . . . no running . . . no pushing . . . no splashing . . . no shouting . . ." —no fun. There's nobody there with a whistle declaring a periodic intermission. You can wear what you want—cutoff jeans seem to be the vogue in our pond—or go "bare naked" if your sense of propriety allows.

The fastidious are repelled by the place, and that usually includes mothers. "Bathers" prefer sandy bottoms or the Mediterranean blue of a chlorinated pool to the tadpoles and cattails of a farm pond. So they don't hang around under the diving board getting in your way. Swimming holes, as a rule, attract swimmers, and they go quite a way toward building swimming skills. It's a matter of survival.

A swimming hole is so totally unsafe that your mom doesn't dare foist your little brother on you, saying, "Look after him." She'll see to it that he learns to swim somewhere else first. The place cannot be reached by telephone, so, though you may catch Hail Columbia when you get home, you can soak for hours there undisturbed. It is not uncommon, of course, for your sister to ride over on her bike and holler out to where you're floating on your inner tube, "You're gonna get it when you get home!"

Another beauty of a swimming hole is that you don't have to spend your Saturday mornings cleaning it. No dragging out the hose and the wand, changing filters, pouring in chemicals. There are no vending machines, so there is almost no litter—an occasional soap wrapper, sometimes a ragged towel or an abandoned inner tube.

It's not the most sanitary place one could swim, I suppose, though I never knew country kids to carry home ear infections as kids do from city pools. Nor, I'm sure, is it the safest place (we have hung up a life buoy purchased at bargain rates from the Soil and Water Conservation Service). But it's close to home, the company's good, and the price is right. And the fun! Doggoned if I don't think I'll go cut the legs off my blue jeans.

Tree Houses

George is building a tree house for his son Grant.

Remember tree houses? Those platforms built from packing crates hoisted by frayed rope into a broad tree crotch? You built them in a burst of energy after lying around a couple of hours on a hot afternoon complaining about how dull life was. The idea struck like lightning when your mom hollered out through the screen door that the chicken house needed cleaning.

The rotting remnants of such a house are rather permanently wedged into an ash tree out beyond our icehouse. The delightful fever of its building is similarly wedged in my memory. When it was finished the boys insisted I crawl up and try it for size . . . or strength, or just to laud their accomplishment. Paul grumbled that the nails involved would be the ruination of the tree.

"Nonsense," I said. He may eventually be proven right. In these fifteen years nobody has crawled up there to remove them. Still, I wouldn't trade the memory for the whole tree.

George's tree house is not of that sort. "You've got to build it sturdy if you want it to support fifteen kids without any lawsuits," he chuckled. "I figure I'll have $350 or $400 invested in it before I'm through."

"Isn't your son helping you?" I asked.

"Well, that was the idea, but his Little League schedule crowds his free time."

My curiosity was aroused, so I stopped by to see this colossus. Sturdy it is, supported by two vertical railroad ties and twelve steel rods bolted through three trees.

With a little crowding—and no fear of lawsuits—it could shelter the Cleveland Browns' offensive and defensive teams. Some might have to spill onto the balcony, but all would be comfortably shielded from the weather and bird droppings by the high-pitched roof. Many could wave burly fists from the several windows. One or two could crowd lengthwise into the loft with its two-by-four flooring.

A neat set of architectural drawings are nailed to the ash tree, which penetrates the floor of the balcony and stretches through the roof. The particle board sheeting has nothing in common with a packing case. The only things this tree house shares with Ted's and Orrin's is that it's off the ground and one of its members is an ash tree.

George's tree house (I hesitate to call it Grant's) is still in the rough stage and has no end of possibilities—cedar shakes, chimney, window boxes, drywall, electricity, plumbing—you get the idea. I think it's a little bit like a geometry problem that "the old man" gets involved with while the kid creeps quietly off to bed.

When George was about Grant's age, he used to climb on my truck on summer mornings and come to End o' Way to pick beans at 25 cents a half bushel. He took the money home at the end of the week and gave it to his mother to keep shoes on his feet and chickens in the pot. By the time he moved on to a job paying minimum wage ($1 an hour), he was our bean champion, picking five bushels on a good morning ($2.50). In his four or five years of working at End o' Way, he probably earned enough to pay for that tree house he's building for his son.

Oh yes, we're still hiring those little bean pickers at End o' Way. They come from good homes like Grant's. But for some funny reason, the days are hotter; the mornings, longer; the bean picking, more difficult. They hit their stride at about a bushel a morning. That yields them two bucks, and any dummy can tell you that's only worth about twenty brisk minutes of Pac Man.

Mistaken Identity

The summer I was nine my brothers John and Bill and I had a rare, two-week holiday with our Uncle Ed and Aunt Edna in a house trailer parked under the Ambassador Bridge in Windsor, Ontario. (Uncle Ed had always been a vagabond, so he took to the house trailer like a naked turtle to a shell.) I was not a perceptive child, and so it didn't occur to me that two weeks of vest-pocket confinement with country kids of eight, nine, and eleven was a dreadful strain on our childless Aunt Edna.

She was as prim and inflexible as one can become whose life has never been cluttered with children or other major challenges. That may account for the happy turn circumstances took in that memorable interval.

John, Bill, and I were drawn like water rats to the Detroit River. Only a trio conditioned in a mud creek would have considered swimming in the oil scum that even in the halcyon thirties coated that busy commercial river. Somehow we managed to climb up and dive off the great cement abutments supporting the bridge, to the alarm of bystanders on shore. We also appropriated a rowboat from somewhere and rowed out into the channel, where tugs and steamers tooted at us as sailors on deck waved in amusement.

Our harried Aunt Edna was back at the trailer struggling to restore order and keep ahead of our youthful appetites, little suspecting what heroics we were up to. A good thing, too!

One hot afternoon when Aunt Edna had settled a fistfight between John and Bill by sending them uptown with nickels to spend, I lolled on the benches that flanked the table at one end of the trailer, rattling on to Aunt Edna about nine-year-old nonsense.

"One place I've always wanted to go is Hollywood," I said.

"I suppose you've heard your Papa talk about it, haven't you? I'll speak to your Uncle Ed when he comes home. Perhaps we can drive up there this weekend."

I furrowed my brow, wondering at what she was saying. She had clearly misunderstood me, and I didn't know how to say so without shattering this misimpression she had. She was obviously pleased at my assumed interest in someplace meaningful to our late father. I said nothing and waited to see what would evolve.

Uncle Ed must have recognized that one more long weekend with these hyper kids was going to send Aunt Edna over the edge. So we went on the weekend . . . to Hollywood? To Holy*rood*, a small Scottish settlement a few miles inland from Lake Huron in Ontario's western reaches.

Our Grandfather Penton's "Cousin Suze," a Marjorie Main sort of maiden lady with a gruff voice and a generous spirit, ran the general store and farm dairy at Holyrood. It was also the local gas station, ice cream parlor, and social center. John and Bill and I were bug-eyed in wonderment. We were not then of an age to take much interest in where our people had come from, so this remote setting from our father's boyhood emerged like a few pages from a mystery story of which we knew neither the setting, the plot, the end, nor the characters.

Much of the charm of the place lay in its being one vast connected unit, the sort of arrangement common in deep snow country. (I presume that the prevailing westerly winds crossing Lake Huron dropped a lot of snow on Holyrood, no doubt still do.) The general store occupied a big room downstairs; the spacious living quarters were on the second floor, an arrangement that seemed strange to us. I have a vivid impression of the darkened Victorian parlor with marble-top tables and horsehair sofas nearly obscured by sofa pillows of satin and velvet. By climbing the enclosed staircase and making our way to the rear of the attic through the welter of antiquities stored there, we emerged in the cavernous haymow of the barn.

The icehouse was another distinct feature of this barn. It was, in fact, a tiny room insulated with sawdust and built into the haymow so that the hay bales could provide further insulation. Access was through a small but very thick door cut into the room low on an outside wall. It was filled with jugs of milk, bowls of butter, crocks of lard, and other country products sold through the general store. Our young minds, unaccustomed to miracles, found it difficult to believe that the ice, cut, they said, from a nearby lake in winter, was still ice in July.

It was a memorable visit indeed, a brief look backward into a world our father had known, that place to which our roots had been transplanted from Scotland and England a century earlier. And it all came about by mistake. Aunt Edna lived on to an age when we were adults together, but I never had the heart to tell her that I hadn't heard of Holyrood until she took us there.

Even now I wonder about the whole episode. Who were the shadowy people who moved through the weekend patting our heads, murmuring, "Harold's children"? What did they really have to do with us, and what ever became of them? I've never gone back in search of Holyrood, Ontario. Is it there at all, or was it merely a place of illusion—like Hollywood?

Brake for Librarians!

Stratford, Ontario: From the moment you spot the Old English script *S* on the water tower on the southwest approach, you know that the ghost of Will Shakespeare hangs over this town. The grain elevator alongside the railroad announces "Co-op" in homelier print, a reminder that this was once a placid farmer town disturbed by nothing more exciting than the Canadian National Railway or the humming of sawmills. That was, of course, before the Bard blew in to a fanfare of trumpets in 1953, initiating a Shakespeare Festival in a tent along the Avon. The festival has become an institution now, with three permanent theaters, a drama school, and dramatics almost year round.

In the mist over the swimming pool on a summer morning you could call up visions of the Three Witches, though no one who hadn't drunk much too much would call it a bleak and lonely heath. The figures are more likely to materialize as three merry wives of Windsor, Ontario, or three widows from Walla Walla on a cultural safari plotted by the AAA.

Stratford probably has more English teachers per square foot than any piece of real estate on the continent. A sign mid-block between gift shops reading, "English Teachers Crossing," would probably go far toward ensuring the future of the language.

There is a place, however, for reluctant husbands dragged unwilling to this cultural watering trough—a golf course is rumored to exist on the "moors" beyond the village. No Shakespearean devotee, of course, has ever seen it. Literary ladies arrive on buses and cluster around picnic tables in the park, discussing the extended metaphors of the day's drama. Or they tour the Gallery Stratford (the art museum) to see Shakespeare as the world's artists have imagined him.

The cosmopolitan crowd at the Queens Hotel will attest that the Ontario Avon flows more clearly than the British Avon; their opinions will vary on the quality of the drama. They will agree that what Stratford, Ontario, lacks in history and authenticity it supplies in convenience and geniality.

There is no lack of shops wherein to spend the longer American dollar. Each has its clever come-on—a catchy name, a distinctive decor, a unique product, a resident artisan. The proprietor himself may be the attraction. The philosophical host of the German china

49

shop might bend your ear with his plan for bringing harmony to Ireland. "Why don't we bring those kids over here by the boatload, put them in Canadian homes, and show them there's a better way of life?"

He tells of having a whole tour of Brazilian students challenge him to a discussion. "Another day one of the performers was in here, and he launched into a soliloquy from Molière. For a whole hour I didn't sell a thing. All we had was theater."

The play, of course, is the thing. You can have *Macbeth* in the afternoon and *Much Ado About Nothing* after dinner, both or neither, as you like it. Or you can sample other classicists, like Voltaire and Strindberg. One man in his time plays many parts. Monday's Melancholy Jacques may on Tuesday speak for Chekhov. Thursday's tragedian may be Friday's fool. Some of the cast enjoy world renown, and others are gifted students in ascendance.

If fitness is your thing, you can jog through the manicured parks that bloom where the Avon widens into Lake Victoria. But matrons in their Dexter walking shoes are in the plurality. Every corner in repose has its pot of petunias or its spikes of delphinium. The orderly gardens are a delight.

The dramatic influence may be English, but the cuisine is principally French. You can consume it in cozy tearooms hung with ferns and chintz, in Victorian drawing rooms draped in velvet, in stone cellars cool with casks, in flagstoned gardens bordered with herbs, or yet in chilly dining rooms of glass and aluminum warmed only by skylights and humorous pink nudes.

The mix of people who converge on Stratford is as rich as the pastry and the plays. From every nation they come with their varied conditioning, their private prejudices. "The last time I saw *Macbeth*," said a retired businessman, "was in the Fiji Islands." And then there was the Viennese chauvinist who told us, "If you really want to read good Shakespeare, you should read it in the German translation. It is marvelous. Better than the original."

Aha! Here at last, the answer to the question that has baffled scholars through the centuries. Who was Shakespeare *really*? A German imposter!

Who would say for sure, then, that the British Stratford isn't merely a counterfeit of this one, this charming, cultural island in the agricultural sea of Ontario?

Corn, Beans, and Bedlam

Bank Street is a sleepy little road with no outlet where a cyclist can "pop a wheely" undisturbed, a dog can stretch to snooze on the warm tar, and frogs will hunker down to croak on rainy nights. But the traffic streaming up this way in August might lead you to think we were running a still. The pick-your-own people are back to glean with their baskets, boxes, and bags, their grandmas and neighbors and in-laws, their kids and dogs and their wondrous enthusiasm.

"This ain't the easiest place in the world to find," says a fellow in an "Almost Heaven, West Virginia" T-shirt, "but it shore is purty. Y'all have half runner beans?"

"These are bush beans," I explain.

"Are they good and full? We wanta cook 'em with a little salt pork and some taters."

I direct him to an older field of beans where he can find what he wants and run to answer the phone.

"Is this the farm where you pick your own corn?" asks a young woman. "How do I get there?" I repeat the instructions that were in the newspaper and go to the kitchen to peel peaches for lunch.

"Ma, there's a lady here with a pot of soup. Says she told you she was gonna bring you some when she came back for corn," hollers Orrin from the front yard. "C'mon out here and take care of her."

By now the phone is ringing again. Out by the mailbox four adults and three kids are crawling out of a beat-up station wagon, mopping their brows, fanning themselves, fishing in their purses for money, dumping corn on the lawn to count it.

"Orrin, get that phone."

"Can you drink the water in the well?" ask the children, as they storm the pump.

The lady with the soup wants to talk. I'm trying to settle up with the people from the station wagon for the corn.

"Tell me again how you make that soup," I say, trying to wax enthusiastic. A dignified older couple arrive in a Lincoln Continental. I wince to think of it gray with country dust. The lady holds a beribboned poodle that starts to yap as she lowers the window.

"Are the beans good and young?" she asks. My Labrador, who had been sleeping beneath the shrubbery, comes charging out to defend her territory and her litter of pups from a poodle with a pink ribbon.

51

The lady hurriedly closes the electric window and secludes her pet in his air conditioning.

"Mom, you're wanted on the phone," calls Orrin from a window.

"We got fourteen dozen here. Can you change a twenty?" say the people with the station wagon.

"I'll just put this kettle in the kitchen," says the soup lady. I murmur my thanks, get the change for the twenty, and go back out front, where my dog is still assaulting the Lincoln Continental. The mailman arrives, blowing his horn and distracting Heidi from the yapping poodle. Meanwhile the station wagon kids have discovered Heidi's pups and add their squeals of delight to the din.

I send the poodle people up the lane in search of young beans just as the serviceman rolls in to repair the refrigerator. Orrin directs him to the kitchen.

My soup lady is back. . . . "Something was boiling over on your stove. I turned the fire down. When you're ready to serve that soup, you thicken it just a little, and you add some vinegar and sour cream."

"The mailman has a C.O.D. for $35.38," hollers Orrin. "Should I pay him?"

A purple minibus pulls in as the people in the station wagon collect their corn and kids and depart. A guy in blue jeans, T-shirt, ponytail, and a cross on a leather thong asks if he can have "a few minutes" of my time.

"If you try really hard," I say. He's selling Bibles.

"Now you'd probably expect to pay at least $150 for a set like this. . . ." The phone rings. Paul and the two boys and our two little houseguests arrive from the bean fields for lunch.

On the phone a man asks, "Are you the people with the pups for sale?"

"Yup. Corn and beans and pups," I say.

Then it's Orrin again in the front yard. "Ma, can you come out here a second?" Having given directions to the puppy customer, I head out front again. My "Almost Heaven" fellow is back.

"I thought you'd want to see his corn," says Orrin with a smile.

"Them shore is big ears," says the fellow, twisting his car key to reveal a trunkful of Charley Schmalz's field corn.

"Shore are," I say, winking at Orrin. "Hope you got a pen of hogs at home to feed 'em to."

Back in the house Ted is fighting his way to the sink, stepping over the repairman lying prone under the refrigerator.

"How's come lunch isn't ready? Yuck! What's this soup?" he says, lifting a lid and casting a jaundiced eye at the Bible salesman, who's nervously collecting his $65 set of books and backing out the door with the terrified air of someone who has just wandered into an asylum.

"I'll pray for you people," he says as he flees for his minibus.

Amazing Grace

A decree went out from the deacons' board that the Sunday school picnic should be held on the first Sunday of August. And Deacon Leimbach being of good heart and weak mind volunteered his little garden of Eden for the festivities.

Verily the week arriveth, and Deacon Leimbach gathered his family around him, saying, "Lo, this place is a mess!" And they girded their loins with strength, and they went into the gardens and the meadows with rakes and hoes and pruning snips. Even unto the ends of the acres goeth the sons with hay choppers and mowers and between them they maketh all things neat.

The neighbor looketh upon this frenzied order and asketh, "What gives?" And when it was explained to him, he went into his yard too and made all things beautiful.

"Here is the place where we shall build the altar," said the good wife, and Deacon Leimbach taketh issue, prophesying heat and small breeze for that spot. The wife protesteth, and the deacon saith loudly, "Have it your way!"

The good wife gathered field flowers in great pitchers and set them around her chosen sanctuary. And she setteth up an easel to conceal the rubbish barrel. The sons of the deacon hauleth tables and chairs and hymnals from the church and lo, they groaneth loudly.

The day arriveth and with it the preacher and the deaconess with the communion bread. She setteth the bread upon the telephone cable spool disguised as an altar, and lo the puppy taketh communion, whereupon Deacon Leimbach banisheth the puppy to the shed, where he yelpeth.

At the appointed hour the worshipers came and with them the heat and small breeze and great swarms of flies, and Deacon Leimbach's prophesy was fulfilled.

Deacon Leimbach read from the book of Ephesians in the family

53

Bible set high upon a dictionary stand and invoketh the Lord to his tidy acres. With joyous hearts they worshipeth and shooeth away the thirsty flies as the old dog slept in the center aisle.

"Morning hath broken, like the first morning," sang they lustily, and verily, thought the good wife, it was the first morning the gardens had been without weeds.

Then stretched they long tables under the maple trees, where the strong breeze bloweth. The women spread cloths and setteth out casseroles and cakes and other fruits of their Saturday afternoon. They praised the Lord in song and fell upon the feast. And God looked down and saw that it was good, and the congregation also.

When the feast was cleared, Deacon Bell announced the games. They accosted one another with balloons filled with water, and all were splashed with laughter and with joy. Then into great potato sacks each of two putteth one leg, and together they ran to a place that was appointed. Deacon Leimbach and his good wife runneth with the rest, and like a ton of bricks fell they down and winneth not the race.

Then the skies grew dark and a great wind blew from the west. The multitudes swept up their picnic baskets and folded swiftly chairs and tables. And into the house and garage and their automobiles went they, pursued by the thirsty flies. And the rains fell.

Deacon Leimbach sitteth upon his porch and looketh across his gardens, strewn now with twigs and leaves and corn fodder from the fields. And he sighed and saw that the Lord answereth prayer for lo, he needeth rain.

Disorientation

When my mother enrolled as a student at the state university in 1912, she packed her petticoats and camisoles in a brass-bound trunk that her father loaded on the box wagon and hauled to the depot in Latty, Ohio. I have a warm vision in my mind of Grandpa and Grandma Musselman standing on the platform waving handkerchiefs as the train chugged off, carrying their bright and headstrong daughter in mysterious directions. They made the trip to and from the depot a number of times in the years that followed, but that was as close as they came to involving themselves in her life at the university. (Perhaps they took the train down themselves for graduation, but who would have done the chores?)

I had occasion to ponder the wisdom of that detachment one recent summer as Paul and I, along with hordes of other freshmen parents, traipsed around the university like displaced persons, getting answers to questions it hadn't occurred to us to ask. We were instructed, for example, in the proper way to chain a bicycle to a fence so that neither fence nor bicycle could be stolen. We were comforted in the knowledge that if our daughter or son were attacked on campus and merely managed to knock the receiver from the hook of the safety alert phones, a patrol car would be on the scene within minutes.

We were assured that if our son or daughter found that his or her roommate was shacking up with his or her paramour in their dormitory room, disciplinary steps would be taken. We were reassured that if emergency surgery were necessary for our son or daughter and his or her parents could not be reached, the matter would not be carried all the way to the AMA before action was taken. We were advised that items of value frequently disappear from dormitory rooms. (So much for the digital watch, the electric typewriter, the Apple II, the portable TV, the stereo, and the microwave oven that Ted keeps telling us are indispensable to the winning of a college degree.)

We were herded into buses and given a tour of the billion-dollar facility. We were ushered through the sophisticated media center, rich in electronic gadgetry. We were invited to "talk" with a computer, who asked if it might call us by our first names. We were encouraged to clamp on headphones and dial-a-lecture from the university tape bank. We were given a demonstration biology presentation coordinating slides and tapes and microscopes. One of the more stimulating professors was tapped to do an oral report on his years of research watching glaciers melt.

We were housed student-wise in dormitory rooms, sterile and cold in their summer abandonment. We struggled with the occupied-unoccupied sign on the door of one bathroom serving four couples.

Why did we go? Orrin, of course, was led to believe that he would fail miserably in his student years if his parents flunked orientation. We knew better.

It just never occurred to us not to go. Mollycoddling is such a way of life in America that we too are caught up in it, though each of us in our student years survived—even prospered—without the long shadow of a hovering parent.

Perhaps it was nostalgia for our lost youth. Alas, today's campus is a world so alien that only our son and his contemporaries will feel at home there. (When a computer tells me my message is rejected, I take it personally.) Perhaps we were trying to compensate for the pampering our parents never gave us. Perhaps we thought we'd make some stimulating social contacts. But we came away reminded that freshman parents don't necessarily have anything more in common than freshmen and college fees.

Our two-day orientation (charge, $60) probably cost us more than Mother paid for a whole semester back in 1912. But it did serve to explain and underscore one disturbing fact about our son's college education—that fees are high and getting higher.

Banner Performance

Strung up in my kitchen is a sagging hanger draped with purple-and-gold banners reading, "Reserve Champion Dairy Kid," "Best of Show," "Jr. High Point Pig," "Grand Champion Fowl," etc. Orrin is on the phone consulting committee members about what banners will be needed in addition to these to properly recognize Lorain County Junior Fair participants.

My opinions are not being solicited, of course, but I can think of some categories of achievers at a county fair who are never recognized with ribbons to hang above their beds or stars to dangle from their crowns.

How about a Grand Champion award for the extension agent who has the six-months' headache of engineering a junior fair? Or a Best of Class banner for the Senior Fair Board member who takes the most guff without losing his cool?

There ought to be a Good Shepherd award, it seems to me, for the guy who sells a lamb to a fledgling 4-H-er for a fraction of its worth, and a Number One Nice Guy award for the butcher who buys it six months later for ten times what it's worth.

Competition would be keen for a Doggone Good Neighbor banner intended for the fellow with the pickup truck who hauls his neighbor's girl's pigs to the fair and afterward cleans the truck himself.

I also favor a Grand Dad award for the father who did the chores when Junior had football practice, Little League, 4-H camp, Farm

56

Bureau meetings, and trombone lessons, and a Miracle Mom award for the mother who took seven girls to fourteen fabric stores on three consecutive afternoons, transported twelve display boards (all with tacky varnish), and mastered the rudiments of electricity, small engines, and rope without putting into practice her skill with a hangman's noose.

There is another category of distinctions that might be honored with cheers—those who add much of the color, the character, the fun to the county fair: Outstanding Line Crasher award to the 4-H-er who hassles everybody in the food tent with regularity (his cow is about to calve, his horse just bit a judge, his chickens are loose . . .).

A Pushiest Prevaricator award for the guy who collects the most pit passes for the demolition derby.

Jr. High Point Pack Rat for the kid who goes home with the most politicians' shopping bags full of matchbooks, rulers, pencils, yardsticks, balloons, stickers, and ballpoint pens.

There is room for a Top Sneak award for the cool cat who gets into the most grandstand shows without paying.

And a Grand Champion Trotter award to the mama who scurries to the fair office fastest to protest the judging. "Now, my Georgie . . . !"

Nobody would want to overlook the campers, an important segment of today's county fair scene. Why not a Grand Champion Slob award for the "gypsy" whose lot most nearly simulates the county dump?

A Best of Show award might be reserved for the well-scrubbed, neatly groomed child who changes his underwear daily and goes home well-rested at week's end with money in his pocket. He won't have had any fun, but he deserves something for doing as his mother advised.

Autumn

Autumn came down in the night with the wind across the orchard,
Easily, far-forth, deliberate, brilliant with anvil flare:
Pouring the crucible wealth of June out of the tortured
Leaves that we quietly stir now and trample in the morning air.

—David McCord, "Oversonnet"

Meanwhile in Ithaca . . .

It was Ulysses, I believe, who first devised the idea of separate vacations for husbands and wives. You will remember from third-year Latin, perhaps, that he went off on a ten-year Odyssey, leaving Penelope with the slaves and the chariots and the drachmas to look after the villa. You will remember too that a few of the local fellows, concerned that Penelope might be lonely, kept trying to seduce her. She held them at bay for years by saying she had this piece of weaving to finish first, but every night she ripped out what she'd woven that day.

My Ulysses went on a two-week odyssey to Sweden one September (to an international motorcycle race with son Ted), and I don't think the local fellows even noticed I was alone. It's just as well, since I'm not into weaving.

The chaos that greeted me daily, however, often made me think somebody had been up nights "unraveling" whatever it was I had accomplished the previous day. Paul did very thoughtfully provide supplemental activity for my spare time. He left me with several bushels of pears to can. If you didn't wince, you've never canned pears!

Taking separate vacations used to be an early warning that a marriage was foundering. Practical farm couples recognize that it's one of the simpler ways to run a farm and still get a vacation, especially in the summer season. In fact, nothing does more to secure a marriage than abandoning the whole place to a wife for a fortnight. Numerous things come into focus. Indeed, in the name of good sense, it should be mandatory that every woman assume total responsibility for a family, home, and business from time to time.

The initial impact was of emancipation. Whoopee! No tight schedule. Go to town and come home whenever. . . . Take the whole day. Visit the museum. Stay for lunch. Look up an old college friend, et cetera.

In a day or two the thrill of this freedom was dulled by the weight of obligations a farm naturally imposes. It wasn't Paul, after all, who demanded a schedule. With all these flights into foolishness things were deteriorating.

Those pears were beginning to take on color.

Then small things began to annoy me. Nobody wound the alarm clock, and there was a frantic morning. The workers were here for orders and I was still in bed. The buttons on the alarm, I discovered, defy manipulation with arthritic fingers. I settled down in the middle of the bed to find that the mattress slants slightly in the direction of "Ulysses' " absent form. I rose in the night to put socks on my cold feet. I understood now why the African violet blooms with such ebullience. Ulysses had been caring for it. The newspapers were stockpiling in the paper box. It was nice to have meals that were flexible, but food never disappeared. The leftovers were getting moldy in the refrigerator.

Only a week and a half and he'd be home. Better get busy on those pears.

Policy decisions began to plague me. Was that field of sweet corn ready to pick? Was it good enough to market if we did pick it? Who would get up in the night and take it to the commission house? Who else?

One more week and he'd return. I rushed around and canned a few of those pears.

Terribly dry. Should we irrigate the potatoes? Or was it too late in the season? Should we kill the vines and get ready to dig? When we'd dug the potatoes, how should we price them?

The bees and yellow jackets were zeroing in on those pears.

Where were last year's sales books? Where were the deposit slips, for crying out loud? Such an orderly desk and I couldn't find a thing!

I had scribble marks all through the checkbooks. What had become of that euphoric feeling of freedom?

Only four more days and he'd be here. I was running out of jars for those pears.

I hadn't done any laundry for a week, and Paul and Ted would have a mountain to add to this when they came home. While a canner of pears was processing, I scurried to the cellar, sorted the clothes, filled the washer, picked up a glass measure, and reached for the soap. There on the top of my box of Tide coiled an enormous black snake! I uttered a primal scream that must surely have resounded through the Swedish fjords. I dropped the glass, dashed headlong up the stairs, out the door, across the porch, and tripped over a crate of those darned rotting pears!

If I'd been Penelope, that's the night I'd have finished the weaving.

Fledging

For three weeks now Paul and I have been stirring the feathers about in our empty nest, waiting for the world to collapse as all the sociologists would have us believe it will. Orrin has gone off to study agriculture with his brother Ted at Ohio State, and we are alone.

It isn't a case of being alone again. We moved into this house the week our first baby was born, twenty-eight years ago, having lived previously with the in-laws. If this was to have been our honeymoon cottage, the honeymoon is long overdue.

There are indeed measurable changes. Our food bills have diminished; our phone bills have increased. Behind us are the hurry-worry mornings. The school bus comes and goes, and we are unconcerned. The clutter is gone and the beds are always made. One week's cleaning runs into another's, and we ask ourselves if we should bother. We turn out the lights at reasonable hours, content that everyone is home. Hassles are down to a minimum. And with the passage of three weeks, I am able to conclude that it isn't really difficult to forgo a state of being that you never really completely embraced.

On a scale of one to ten, I suppose my kids would give me an eight or nine as a mother. But what do they know? They've only had one mother. I had a mother and a mother-in-law. I am a mother. I've read books on motherhood and been a dedicated mother-watcher. This study and experience didn't do much to improve my performance as a mother, but it did make me very conscious of my own failings.

None of the things I did for the children do I regret. What leaves an ache in the heart are the things I never quite accomplished. My earliest failing was with infant vitamins. Somewhere in the back of the refrigerator, I'm sure, are the bottles of infant vitamins that I neglected to give to my infant sons. Dr. Spock cautioned that a lack of vitamins could result in reduced body size.

Fortunately for me, my kids are of the persuasion that their failings are of their own making. They think the reason they weren't basketball stars was that they didn't train vigorously enough. I know that it was vitamins. And those studies that equate success with height scare the liver out of me.

Breakfast was another failing of mine. Indelible is the image of Dane at four on his knees on the counter breaking eggs into a skillet. "See, Mom," he said. "I can cook my own breakfast." I was always a slow starter, and often by the time I got wound up in the morning, the boys were going out the door.

Laundry, too, was short suit. Three or four times through the years I managed to get it up from the cellar and into the drawers. For the most part the boys equated it with hide-and-seek.

I was not always in the house when they came bursting in at the end of the day. Sometimes their supper was late, and sometimes I abandoned them to their father's care. There were even times when we had to move their birthday celebrations to more convenient days.

Some of the years of their lives are unrecorded in the photo albums. The decorating schemes that they designed for their bedrooms were never completely executed—no wallpaper with rocket ships and draperies printed with Snoopies.

And now they are gone. . . .

It took them half an hour to throw their things together and load the car (which must say something about the kind of mother they had). In a last, pathetic gesture I went out and took their photo, as if in that final hovering act I might compensate for the forgotten vitamins, the unpressed shirts, the unmatched socks, the frantic breakfasts, the cold suppers—the collected longings of a haphazard mother.

One secure thought comforts me: No one will ever be able to say that I sent them into the world unprepared to care for themselves.

Beyond Valium

According to the Census Bureau, 50 percent of the American population has moved in the past eight years. Consider the psychological cost of all those moves! No wonder the buzzword of our decade is *stress*. It was inevitable that sooner or later I would catch up with the stress workshops, and sure enough . . .

Our calm, collected leader picked our brains on the subject of personal stress. I'd never really thought of my life as stressful, but after two hours of taking in everybody else's problems, I could hardly wait to get out of there and find somebody with a Valium.

We were advised that these stresses must be exorcised if we were to be functioning individuals. I came home determined to deal with what I had identified as the source of my stress. It's all pretty well hidden in closets and drawers and cupboards—disorganization, the plague of my life.

The next day, as luck would have it, I spoke for a group that was having a workshop session on getting organized! I hung around after I'd delivered my own chaotic lecture to see what I could learn. There were test questions to determine the seriousness of your disorganization.

I flunked them all: 1. "Does it take you more than ten minutes to lay your hand on a given item in your household?" I hid a gold nugget someplace in my house three years ago and haven't seen it since. 2. "Are there papers on your desk you haven't looked through in a week or more?" There are papers on my desk that were mailed with 6-cent stamps. 3. "Do you put off doing a job so long it becomes an emergency or panic situation?" Is there some other way?

I didn't stay for the whole session. Halfway down the list of remedies I read, "Decide to start changing right away . . . while you are motivated." The adrenaline started flowing and the stress was mounting. I sneaked out and raced home (120 miles in two hours).

"Where are you going in such a hurry?" said Paul as I rushed past him and upstairs.

"Gonna clean the bathroom cupboard," I called back.

"What? At 10:30 at night?"

"I'm motivated," said I.

"You're nuts," said he, shuffling off to bed through the chaos of what had been an orderly bathroom ten minutes earlier.

At 3:00 in the morning I was still standing in the bathtub rummaging through the medicine cupboard built above it, trying to figure out whether I would ever really need a quart of Epsom salts, two cans of boric acid, and that Preparation W for the eradication of warts. And Green Mountain Salve for boils! I haven't had a boil for twenty-five years . . . but you never know. And what's this? Kwell medicinal shampoo? The label says, "Indicated for treatment of head lice and crab lice and their nits." Crabs! Oh my gosh, I thought that was just sailor talk! What's *that* stuff doing in here?

There were just too many decisions for that hour of the night. My stomach was one big nervous lump. The root of all this stress is the fact that in all our lives we've never moved. People who move don't harbor things like camphor and Calomine lotion and White Cloverine Salve. They certainly don't keep shampoo for infestations nobody's ever had!

Way back behind the Milk of Magnesia, the green tin of Bag Balm for cow's udders, and the enema syringes was a small plastic pack containing a goggle defogging cloth. Nobody's ever going to use that again, says I to myself, tossing it toward the wastebasket, where it landed with a strange clunk. Hmm . . . that's funny.

I retrieved and opened it. Out rolled my gold nugget! Enough organization for one night. I took a couple of Rolaids and went off to bed.

Did Ya Get the Picture?

Most of the problems with being a farm wife stem from the fact that there is no manual of procedure. It's just a lifelong struggle of on-the-job training. Once upon a time in a blind moment of passion you said, "Yes! Oh yes, I'd love to be a farm wife!" And there you are, fifteen, twenty, twenty-five years later, huddled in a cast-off coat of the kids', a stocking cap pulled low on your brow, trying to figure out what in the heck are the "international farm distress signals."

We usually go through this charade at End o' Way during the potato harvest. Paul is over there on his International 886 pulling a gigantic green machine that's digging up the potatoes, which come spewing out on a moving web. I am moving alongside him on a lesser tractor (with a different gear ratio) pulling a wagon and trying to catch them. There is obviously a wide margin for error here, and being married to a fellow for thirty years is no guarantee you can drive in tandem with him all day without a few skirmishes—mostly verbal.

He's signaling you across the gulf of noise and diesel fumes that separates two tractors, and distress is obvious. You do, of course, learn to read these signs through the years, but the same sign can have several different meanings, so you have to be very good at nuances.

He's half sitting, half standing at the wheel of his tractor, for example, frantically and repeatedly pushing both hands to the side of him. It looks like the maneuver you used to execute down at the goal line when you were a harebrained cheerleader, and it was accompanied by wild shouts of "Go! Go! Go!"

This could be interpreted as meaning that you should drop the wagon at the other end of the field. It could also mean that the hogs are loose. Or he might be trying to say, "There's a banker coming up the lane! Head him off!"

Or—he's sitting placidly at the wheel, a look of disdain on his face, and stretching an arm at full length to the rear. He might be trying to tell you, "You're coming on a little too fast!" But he could just as easily be saying, "If you'd turn around, you knucklehead, you'd notice you lost the wagon."

Some of my farmer's signals are merely conversational, but they are no less baffling. He points overhead. It can mean, "It looks like rain," or "Check out that flock of geese," or "The Feds are up there checking on us with a whirlybird!"

These signals are just as individual as the farmers who issue them, and that's why we need a manual to standardize the language. There are a couple that any farm wife can interpret clearly, however. You are carving a turn at the end of the field, and you take a pass beneath a low-hanging tree limb. He convulsively bends at the waist and grasps his stomach with one hand, his head with the other. Though this may look like a gallbladder attack to the untutored eye, to the farm wife who's lived with it, it says, "You dingbat! I just welded that muffler yesterday!"

Or in any difficult circumstance where you are the offending party and you see a farmer tear off his cap, throw it down, and stomp on it, you can make book on what's going through his head: "If all the machinery weren't in your name, I'd divorce you tomorrow!"

Wish You Were Here

You visit a lot of grand places when you speak to farm groups—Grand Island, Grand Rapids, Grand Junction, Grand Prairie—but now and then you hit a glamorous watering hole, usually in the off season.

It was ten below zero when I spoke in Estes Park. At Myrtle Beach I was besieged by torrential rains. The Ozarks were deep in April slush. Hot Springs, Georgia, in July or Arrowwood, Minnesota, in March did not inspire four-color spreads in *Travel* magazine.

Now and then, though, you luck out—a sun-lovely October day in Daytona Beach!

Picture a corner room on the eleventh floor of the Plaza Hotel: two balconies, east and south, sliding doors open, sea breezes blowing. Ahhh. . . .

I leaned on my railing, looked out toward Africa, up toward Greenland, down toward Cuba—blue sky, bluer ocean all the way. I thought about my first holiday in Daytona . . . the moth-eaten motor court across the causeway, Chef Boy-ar-Dee spaghetti heated in a thin aluminum saucepan over an erratic hot plate, visiting friends in a high-priced motel on the beach, the forbidden pleasure of swimming in their pool. The only things we could afford that year were the generous beach, the free ocean, and the children's unbridled enthusiasm. . . . How the little boys would have enjoyed *this* room.

I descended to the beach then from my elegant lookout. That I had no alternative but to take an elevator is symptomatic of all that has gone awry with man and nature. To reach the wonders of an ocean beach, one should have to struggle down a precipice, climb a barricade of driftwood, or, at the very least, trudge over a sand dune and suffer a few sand burs. Without pain or strain I exited by the rear door onto the hard-packed sand of auto racing legend.

Then up and down the strand, waves washing over my feet, sand dissolving beneath the toes' grip, kelp rolling in the surf. An egret and I eyeballed each other, each thinking the other a queer bird.

I met a friendly old couple who warned me about stepping on the seaweed: "It's soaked with tar from the oil spills." I stirred a piece about with my toe. It wasn't soaked with tar. He scolded me. "Aha! Like a child, you must see!" Then we talked about ourselves.

"We went to Miami for years, but we wouldn't take it now if you gift-wrapped it," they told me. "There are no more open spaces. You

might as well be in New York City. You can't get near the beach."
So now they had settled in Daytona.

"Was it cold up North?" (Florida has greater appeal for northern
transplants when it's cold up North.)

"Is your husband with you?"

"No," I replied. "My husband is home in Ohio digging the last of
the potato crop."

My thoughts shifted northward, to the last five acres over on the
Schuster place. I recalled the glory of the spring morning we finished
planting them, the sweet smell of the blackberry in bloom. Now the
ivory berries would hang on the poison ivy at the fringe of the woods
where the rows ended. A few gold leaves would cling to the tops of
the sycamores, and the oaks would be turning a burnished red.

I remembered that final day of harvest last year when the axle
broke on the digger, and Paul . . . so forlorn. Now he was struggling
there without me while I splashed about in the Daytona surf.

The sun went under a cloud, and the temperature dropped thirty
degrees.

End o' Way Ant

Six hundred years before Christ a fellow named Aesop had a neighbor
something like Ed. When he wrote his impressions of this guy it
came down through the ages as "The Grasshopper and the Ant."

Ed farms with us summers (the rest of the year he's a school ad-
ministrator). He and his family share this remote cul-de-sac with Paul
and me, and so, if we observe anybody, we observe each other. All
fall I've watched him.

On golden afternoons in October, when distant golf courses were
bathed in beckoning splendor, Ed was out there on the playground
with his car hoods up, his manuals out, and his tools spread neatly on
grease cloths along the fenders checking points and plugs, wires and
terminals, water level in the batteries, antifreeze in the radiators, air
in the tires, oil in the crankcases.

He was attended on both sides by his troop of pretty daughters—
however reluctantly—fetching and carrying, waxing and polishing,
holding or handing a tool, at least observing that there's more to
owning an automobile than starting the engine.

On other crisp autumn days they were back and forth to the woods, Ed and his comely females, with the wagon and the chain saw, the wedges and the sledge. Ed has a woodpile so high he can hardly see down to the Pritchetts'—a veritable China Wall of wood.

In due time a roll of snow fencing appeared over on the playground and on an appointed Sunday was set strategically in position. Up in Ed's attic, I feel sure, there is plastic stapled around the windows. Ed's snow shovel is on a hook just inside the back door. The storm windows, of course, are up. He knows where he can lay his hands on a flashlight and rock salt. Pipes near windows have been painstakingly wrapped, holes have been caulked, the furnace has had a good going-over, the oil tank has been checked and double-checked. Ed is ready.

I'm not sure what Ed's been observing. He did comment, as un-critically as possible, that he didn't think it would hurt "those fellows" to drag up a few trees and build a reserve of firewood for the "old folks," meaning us. It was probably one of those "any Sundays" when our sons were out doing whoop-dee-doos on the motorcycle trails.

I harbor a suspicion that there's a lot of corrosion around my battery cables, and when was I not a candidate for fuel line freeze up? I know darned well nobody crawled under the house to wrap the cold water pipe that has frozen the past two winters. The snow shovel has been hauled off to the potato barn. The drifts will blow where they will, emergencies will arise, and we'll face them as we've always faced them, with emergency measures.

We have not spent the autumn singing and dancing and playing the fiddle, exactly. We drained the pumps, poured antifreeze here and there, and got together a stopgap stack of wood, but for a polar alert, we'd never pass muster. We do have one ace in the hole: we've got one great, generous, compassionate neighbor. When Aesop's fabled grasshopper went crying around to the ant's house in the winter of his discontent, he got the word p.d.q. "Bug off, you lazy son of a gun. You knew the winter was coming same as I did."

When the day comes at End o' Way that the barometer falls, the winds rise, and the blizzard gathers, a form will appear out of the void and a reassuring voice will ask, "Everything okay over here? A frozen water pipe? Hold on. I'll be right back with my blowtorch."

In Promotion of the General Welfare

I see by the papers that apple pie is on the wane. It isn't difficult to predict the consequences of its demise. The family is already in decline and the home imperiled. The nation will inevitably go down the tubes. Normally I feel powerless in these national crises, but I think this is one I can handle.

I've always taken a measure of pride in my pies. Perhaps they're not the best-looking ones on the pie table at church suppers, but tastewise I'll stack 'em up against anybody's. A good fruit pie ought to be full enough, it seems to me, that some of the filling has boiled through the crust and left a juicy puddle on the low side, something the cook can dip her finger into on the way over to the church. It should have a golden glaze on its crust and be at least as flaky as the ding-a-ling who baked it.

If I can contribute to the stability of the nation by sharing my pie recipe, I feel duty-bound to do so. Orrin long ago demonstrated for me that it's the recipe and not the talent that produces a good pie. He baked his first pie alone in the kitchen on a Sunday morning when he was fourteen. I was "close to death" up in the bedroom when he came to consult me. "How do you make pie crust?" he asked. Because I was too weak to protest disaster, I simply gave him the recipe:

> Put 3 cups of sifted flour in a bowl with ½ teaspoon salt;
> Cut in 1 cup of lard (should be room temperature) with a pastry blender until particles are pea size. ("Pea size" is one of those judgments you learn to make strictly on your own alone with "alum the size of a walnut" and "a brine that can float an egg.")
> Gradually stir in with fork ½ cup milk.
> Work into ball with hands. Pinch off portions a bit smaller than a baseball and roll out on a floured pastry cloth. (A pastry cloth and a rolling pin sleeve simplify the rolling process considerably.)

He returned in a couple of hours with a dandy apple pie. The crust was a little thick in spots, but it was every bit as flaky and tender as his Grandmother Penton's (whence came the recipe).

I've discussed this crust recipe with several good cooks who use it, and we conclude that milk is the key ingredient. It prevents that sickly pallor from which pies often suffer. But more important, it

71

produces a tender crust even if you botch it and have to moisten and reroll the dough a couple of times. Strangely, all the cookbooks I've consulted still advocate ice water. Good old country cooks prefer lard as the shortening, something to do, I'm sure, with those tubs of the stuff produced at one time by hog butchering. Vegetable shortening makes a decent pie too—as long as you use that milk as the moistening ingredient.

Any good cookbook can supply proportions for a variety of pie fillings, but since I'm out to save the country, I'll carry through with the apple. I happen to live in an apple region, so I get a choice of varieties, but you'll have to use the cooking apple available in your area. No apple, I am persuaded, will make a bad pie. I like Jonathans because they don't get mushy, and it's hard to beat the old Staymen Winesap. Mother's favorite was always the Baldwin, but nobody who remembers the Baldwin and can still *find* it will have read this far in the pie recipe of an upstart! The apple growers and produce people will have other suggestions.

Pastry for 9-inch double crust

6 or 7 cups apple slices
¾ cup sugar (or a pinch extra for more or tarter apples)
3 tablespoons flour
1 teaspoon cinnamon or more, to taste
¼ teaspoon nutmeg
¼ teaspoon salt
1 or 2 tablespoons butter or margarine dotted over apples

When you've moistened the rim of the lower crust and sealed in the apples with the top crust (well-ventilated with slits), *don't forget that glaze.* Mix a teaspoon of milk with a tablespoon of sugar and smear it over the upper crust.

The pastry recipe will make two double-crust pies if you roll it thin. By cutting the fringes off those, moistening them slightly, and rerolling, you can eke out an eight-inch single crust. Bake one, freeze the other two, and you'll have harmony around the house for a month or so. (Never feed them so much pie that it ceases to be a treat!)

Bake that apple pie at 425 degrees for forty or fifty minutes or, if you're doing a roast at 350 degrees, just bake the pie alongside till it's good and brown and running all over the oven. (Pies aren't particular about their baking temperature.) When there's a cloud of black smoke pouring out of the oven vent and somebody out front hollers, "What's on fire?" your pie's probably done.

They Also Serve

Several years ago I bought a crewel embroidery kit for my mother. Some months later she returned it barely begun, her few stitches in a tangle. With it was a sad note in her graceful script expressing regret that she could no longer discipline her fingers to the complexities of needlework. "I don't know why this is happening to me. I have tried so hard to avert this deterioration by living a good, healthful life." It was the only indication she ever gave that she knew her capacities were betraying her.

Once she passed that point of recognition, the sadness lessened. As late as a year ago, when she was eighty-six and could no longer remember two thoughts in succession, she sat in my kitchen talking abstractly of the time when she would be old and might have to go to a "rest home." "But I don't suppose I will know by then where I am, and it won't much matter."

Mama played life by all the rules, as she understood them. She worked hard; she was scrupulous about nutrition; she stimulated her mind with all manner of food for thought; she devoted her life to her family. She has succeeded in living longer than any of her parents or grandparents, but without the keen presence of mind that made her such a vital woman. Our fate in old age seems after all to be determined by some absurd lottery. For five years, after she could no longer care for herself, Mama lived with my sister, my brothers, and me, moving at two-week intervals from home to home, growing more and more confused and disoriented.

She sits in her wheelchair now at the nursing home, in the clean and shapeless garments that are the indistinction of such a place. She has neglected to put in the teeth that were always a point of pride with her. "Can't understand why folks complain about false teeth. Mine never gave me a moment's trouble," she would say every morning when I cleaned them.

She can't identify me specifically, but she knows in a vague way that I am familiar. "Oh, I didn't know you were coming today. I'm so glad to see you. I hope you brought some money so I can pay them for my care. They'll be coming by for me, won't they?"

"Yes, dear, they'll be coming by."

"Well, I'll be waiting."

Waiting is the preoccupation of rest home inmates. They do not rest; they wait. You enter the lobby with trepidation. All eyes turn upon you, and you know they are waiting. Then you experience both relief and deflation, knowing it is not you for whom they wait. Even Mama, though she is happy to see me, claims to be waiting for "them."

Conversation is forlorn and difficult in Mama's wing, as it is nearly everywhere in a rest home. If minds are not vacant upon arrival, they soon become so. Perhaps that is why people find easy excuses to avoid these places. Most of us are poor at monologue, ill at ease with our own voices.

Sometimes I take my embroidery and just sit quietly sewing beside her. It is as if she were back in her easy chair by the dining room window, and I am her little girl struggling over my sampler. Today I have brought a book to read aloud, *Charlotte's Web*, a children's book chosen as much for my pleasure as hers.

She is disinterested at first, but as the story proceeds, she smiles and nods and chuckles sometimes, relating as the farm girl she was to the little girl with the pet pig and the fanciful talking spider. Now I am her mother, and she is the little girl being read to beside the register at bedtime.

My eyelids grow heavy and my tongue becomes thick. I put aside the book and curl up on her bed. She reaches out to pull a blanket over me and lets her hand rest on my hair.

"You'll look after me, won't you, Mama?" I say.

"Yes, dear, I'll look after you," she replies, and a sort of radiance envelops her.

In that sleepy moment I recognize what it is that they all await.

Celebration of a Life

The day my father died is more distinct in my mind than the day before yesterday. There was an ominous silence on the school bus. Kids whispered to each other, and some little girl said to John, "Your dad died," and some bigger child said, "Shhh!" And we were all quiet, embarrassed, unbelieving.

We got off the bus and straggled up the lawn, with none of the usual jubilant racing to the door. Mother wasn't there. Instead, Aunt Edna met us and said, "Have you heard the message?" The tiny thread of hope gave way, and we drifted to the corners of the house to cry alone. I went to the closet in the bedroom and John was there.

I wandered to the kitchen where a communal handkerchief was being kept behind a cupboard door. Hank was weeping into it.

"I don't know what everybody's crying for," said little Bill in confusion. None of us could explain. Eventually, Mama came in the back door carrying two bags of groceries, and things were immediately better. She put her arms around Mary and they wept together. "What are we going to do without him?" Mama sobbed.

She already knew what she was going to do. She would look after her brood—so she brought home groceries. . . .

Forty years later we gathered in Mama's living room to plan a celebration of her life, which drew to a quiet end at eighty-six. The memories flooded back to document the years that followed her anguished question.

Memories of Mama . . . going out at sunset to gather bouquets of asters and zinnias to garnish the next day's market load, rising then before dawn to take her produce to the city in a battered panel truck. We laughed at the thought of Mama in her market apron sobering a customer complaining of prices. "Did you ever try to raise yourself a few peaches?"

She was somehow defined by the work she did—canning tomatoes, hanging out wash, cooking lunch, and writing good cheer to a college son—all simultaneously . . . or washing jugs in the cider mill while Erik made cider, or sorting asparagus with Ted's wife Mabel when the younger children had gone off to school on May mornings.

We resurrected Mama and the Sunday dinner triumph: fried chicken, mashed potatoes and gravy, homemade rolls, and cherry pie. John remembered Mama making room at the breakfast table for one, two, three, or more of his friends who showed up at the morning head count. There was Mama sending us off, one at a time, on a boat or a bus or a train to see what was beyond the horizon. One of my special memories was of Mama's bringing out on my birthday a gift book inscribed, "To my little girl."

Mary and I treasured too thoughts of Mama clutching a small purse of cash while making a triumphant journey to a distant bank to pay off the mortgage, stopping then in a gift shop to buy a piece of china to commemorate the event.

Ted recalled their traveling to California together, with Mama holding a skillet on her lap and saying, "If you can just find a place to stop and build a fire, I'll cook us a little something."

It wasn't all sweet sentiment. There were old wounds, long healed, that grew from her prejudices, her apprehensions: "Did she ever lend her blessings to any of our unions?" said my Hungarian brother-in-law, who bore the burden of redeeming in her sight both the Catholic church and the "foreign element."

"Look at it this way, Frank," said Gunver, our Danish sister-in-law. "You smoothed a path for me." In the end Mama loved them all and was fiercely loyal. Her seven children became fourteen.

"She surely taught me a lot about plants," said Alice.

"Well, she taught *me* a lot about cooking!" said Gunver.

"She taught me a lot about prejudice," laughed Bill. "We're trying to bring our children up with more tolerance."

But nowhere in anyone's reminiscence of her was there a hint of self-pity. She accepted her difficult lot with pride and lived life with remarkable vigor. There were poignant memories of Mama coming up the hill at night with a lantern and a pail of milk; Mama in her one good dress catching a bus to Amherst for the only social event in her month, a meeting of the Study Club; Mama coming up the sidewalk of a college dorm with a bunch of bittersweet and a laundry case of clean clothes . . . warm memories of the generous and vibrant woman who gave us life and guided us to security in it.

Room at the Inn

When you speed out to a place like O'Neil, Nebraska, where you've been told there's only one traffic light, you don't bother to phone ahead for reservations. If there is no motel, which seems likely, the effort would be futile. If there is a motel, it surely isn't going to be full on a weekday afternoon in September.

Already you've made two bad mistakes. The first one is in "speeding" out. Having arrived then, speeding ticket tucked disconcertingly in wallet, you discover that O'Neil is an oasis in a rather sparsely settled desert, and that it has not one motel but five. I'm sure of the number because I visited them all—one, two, three, four, five—and very early on your average weekday afternoon they are all full.

The lady in the fifth motel had sympathy for me in my plight. There was, she cautiously ventured, an old hotel in the center of town, and if I wished, she would call the lady who runs the place. The vision came clear: a down at the heels, turn of the century hotel where the plumbing chatters, the radiators hiss, stained wallpaper peels from crumbling walls, and a sixty-watt bulb hangs from a twelve-foot ceiling. But I needed a bed.

"Would you please?" I said.

"I'll call, but you'll have to talk to her," said the motel lady. "The last time I sent somebody there they didn't show, and the old girl called to tell me I owed her for the room. Here she is. . . ."

I took the phone and asked about a room.

"Who is this?" she asked in a tone better suited to squelching obscene phone calls than to renting a room.

"Well, I'm from Ohio. I'm in town to speak for the Farm Credit meeting tonight." I gave her my name.

"Oh yes," she said, her voice suddenly warming. "I saw your picture in the paper, didn't I? I think I've got one room left."

I presented myself and my credit card a few minutes later in the nondescript lobby of the hotel, on the corner at the traffic light.

"Do you have any cash?" asked the grim old gal at the desk when I offered her my credit card.

"Well, a little. How much is the room?"

"Eight dollars," she said.

It was a small town, but eight dollars! Must really be a fleabag. I paid the eight dollars, took up my suitcase, climbed the stairs, and peered down the dim corridor, squinting in search of room eleven.

I went through the usual key fumbling and opened the door. I was Dorothy awakening in Oz! The room was huge—and bright—and elegant! White walls, powder blue plush carpeting that appeared never to have been stepped upon, French Provincial furniture in white—a king-sized bed, a large armoire, a dainty writing desk, a blue velvet chaise lounge. The windows were draped in white organza, and cheerful oil paintings of flowers hung on the walls. I was so delighted that I called the only person I knew in town to effervesce —the lady at motel number five.

I wallowed in the luxury of the place—did my exercises in the radiance of the afternoon sunlight flooding onto the plush carpet, worked on my correspondence at the little writing desk, relaxed to read on the blue velvet chaise—a sybarite at last!

On my way out that evening, I stopped at the desk to express my deep pleasure to the innkeeper. At that moment two men with briefcases entered the lobby.

"Do you have a room?" one asked.

"No, nothing," said the woman.

"Well, what would you suggest?" asked the second man.

"There are five motels in town," she said with a condescending air. "You could try them."

"Don't bother," I said, putting my foot in my open mouth. "They're all full. I checked."

"Well!" said my innkeeper, drawing herself up indignantly. "If I'd known that, I never would have given you the Governor's Suite." And then to twist the knife a bit she added, "No sir! I wouldn't have."

Unfortunately, no trapdoor opened to swallow me. I could only stand there, two feet tall, stammering.

That was ten years ago, and I have fumbled with hundreds of motel and hotel keys since, never without a flicker of hope that this room will be another Governor's Suite . . . but it never is. Alas, innkeepers are on to me. They know an ingrate when they see one.

Son of the Middle Border

My fetchin' up was not weighted heavily to the fine arts. A faded print of *The Horse Fair* hung on the wall over brother Erik's crystal set, and *The Gleaners* bent to their eternal labor above the library table. Some grade school art teacher taught me to identify *Pinky* and *The Blue Boy*, but that was about it for art. Even living in the shadow of the Cleveland Museum of Art during my university years did little to school me in art appreciation. All that homework. . . . I go often now to museums, trying to recoup, responding to a little of this and that, sometimes wondering what I should be looking for and what I should be feeling.

Once when I was in Brookings, South Dakota, a friend who wanted to share the indigenous culture took me to the art center of South Dakota State University to see "the Harvey Dunns. You know Harvey Dunn, of course?"

"Oh, of course," I stammered. I lie a lot for art's sake. Now, here in this collection of magnificent South Dakota paintings was art to which I could fully relate. What was so compelling?

In my travels speaking for farm groups in recent years I've spent a lot of time in the Middle Border (the Dakotas, Nebraska, Minnesota, and Wisconsin) and had ample time to muse on its sun-bleached structures, to delight in tiny windmills moved by omnipresent winds,

78

to ponder the dramatic skies and their clean meeting with the earth. I have picked sunflowers along the roads and gathered nosegays of clover and alfalfa.

One afternoon I drove a mile off the highway along a rutted lane, climbed a fence and up a hill through prairie grass to an abandoned graveyard miles and miles from any human source. I have spent time with the rural people, wondered at their courage, and heard them speak with pride of stoic forebears.

And all the while I strove to create in my mind's eye pictures against this backdrop of those homesteaders doing the things I knew they did, supporting each other, surviving the rigors, dreaming the dreams required to endure, loving this prairie, or moving on.

Now here they all were on the walls of this museum, those pictures of my imagining, painted by Harvey Dunn, a son of the Middle Border who went East and made it big as an illustrator for the *Saturday Evening Post*. Harvey traveled the world and painted what his assignments called for, grew rich, and won influential friends. But his heart belonged to the prairie, where he returned during summer holidays to paint what he knew best. This collection is his legacy to prairie people.

Here came the settlers in their half-covered wagons in search of milk and honey. In time it would flow from the waving grasses. Here they were clearing the land, loading stones on a stone boat,* plowing under buffalo bones, standing atop the snow that had buried their sod huts in a blizzard. Here were children spilling out of country schools, picking sunflowers with their mothers, bringing home a pheasant for supper.

And the prairie woman—coming home as a bride in an oxcart, the turbulent sky telling as much of her fate as the rude cart and the rutted trail. There she was at her water pump in the parched summer, and again strong and vital with her rake, and here, standing alongside her working husband in silent support. Dakota woman, dreaming on a sunny bluff, umbrella raised over her sleeping baby, at her mailbox hungrily reading letters from home.

Here they were, the old settlers, faces etched by the wind and the living, like the buildings and the landscape behind them. And there they all were in mourning garb, clustered about an open grave among the crosses on my hill, miles and miles from anywhere, under a

---

* An old farm implement that was pulled behind a horse and slid like a boat on the earth, used for the loading and removal of stone.

leaden sky that seemed, like the people, to grieve. *I Am the Resurrection and the Life,* Harvey Dunn called the painting.

Art appreciation proceeds not from a course, I think, but from living and a yearning to understand.

Hard Scrabble

In the course of a two-day seminar I attended in Washington, D.C., in 1980, I heard more than once "what a bore" it is when folks come down there complaining that "farmers are going broke."

"Particularize," said a member of the House Ag Committee. "Bring facts and figures to back up your assertions—specific examples."

I thought of that bureaucrat a few weeks later as I sat at the kitchen table having breakfast with a couple I'll call Bernita and George Dickle, in their 200-year-old farmhouse in Ohio's southern reaches.

"You wouldn't think, to look at those fields, that they'd need to be tiled, would you?" said George. The farm is a succession of rolling fields falling, now steeply, now gently, to the Ohio River.

"No," I said. "Looks like they'd drain themselves naturally."

"But it's all clay, and it hardly drains at all. I got two miles of tile out there in that field." He indicated a contoured swath lying to the west beyond the gravel road that loops up behind the house and leads back to the main highway.

George had come in from morning chores in the feedlot and was waiting for the vet. "Gotta inoculate cattle today. Lost seven of them last spring with infectious bovine rhinitis." He slumped in his chair, his big rough hands cupped about his coffee mug, and talked about farming. He told me about the epidemic of rhinitis, of the prolonged and grueling ministrations to the herd. "Then the vet bill was $1,300!

"Went up to the machinery dealers to price a new tractor. The one I bought for $14,000 four years ago now costs $25,000 . . . the same darned thing! Seems like a farmer never gets out of debt, never any light at the end of the tunnel."

I didn't pry into George's finances. I don't think he's "going broke," but maybe he'd be better off if he did. It seemed to me that even modest prosperity had eluded these two and probably always would.

The house and land had been in Bernita's family for two centuries, and pride in that fact shone through all their depression. They loved these stubborn acres.

"Never had a real vacation. Nobody to look after the cattle. Seems like our holidays take the form of a walk up over the hill. Always come back feeling better," said Bernita. "The children have traveled a lot, though, with FFA, 4-H, and Homemakers."

Two of the Dickle children were studying agriculture at Ohio State. Bernita took a job at their small town bank to help meet college expenses. "That's another thing we're upset about. Jimmy was so enthusiastic and motivated when he was in high school. But some spark has gone out of him at college. Doesn't seem to take any interest in the farm any more."

I thought about Jimmy and about this farm, about the stately old farmhouse remodeled through the years with the few leftover dollars. Maybe Jim had looked around and discovered, as many a country boy has in generations past, that there are easier ways to make a living.

But there are younger boys, seven and twelve. Both are eager little farmers, as is the college daughter. Surely one of the children will take up the cause, for that's what these hard scrabble places are after two or three generations, a family cause. Perhaps one of them will discover the magic key to making a flourishing operation of this marginal farm. I hope so, but the odds are against it.

The pity is that folks like the Dickles can't afford to go to Washington to "particularize" for the bureaucrats.

Soft Touch

According to the limousine driver who took me to the airport, nearly everybody in Philadelphia eats the soft pretzel.

"I bought one once," I said, "but I was disappointed."

"Well, like anything else, there's good ones and there's bad. The good ones are crisp on the outside and soft on the inside. You get a bad pretzel, that's a really bad trip. Some guys keep 'em around too long. Don't sell 'em. They get stale. Or it's a wet day and they get soggy. Federal Pretzel Company makes the best kind."

"So they have to be hard to be good," I summarized.

"No, not hard, crisp. You know, like toast. Fellow don't have much money, he gets a cup a' coffee and a soft pretzel with mustard. Makes a meal."

"Mustard!"

"Oh yeah, ain't anything without mustard. Where ya from?"

"I'm from Ohio. A farm near Cleveland."

"Cleveland, huh. Someplace near the Ozarks?"

"Not too near. The Ozarks are down in Arkansas and Missouri."

"That ain't too far, though."

" 'Far' is relative, I think. I live up on Lake Erie."

"Gettin' to be a swamp, Lake Erie, ain't it?"

"No, not really. Reports of its death are highly exaggerated."

We stopped just then in front of a hotel to await more passengers, and we struck up a conversation about skid row types.

"I got a bunch of 'em on my 'payroll.' Used to give 'em a dime, but they're hittin' me up now for 35 or 50 cents. Everything goin' up in price. Can't blame 'em. Poor old guys. I could show you a bunch of men—women too—carry everything they own around in a paper bag. Live on the street, or flop down at night in a flophouse.

"See that old guy sittin' over there? The one with the white beard? If he spots me, he'll make a beeline over here. Won't even care if he gets hit by a car. He's one of my boys. They all got me spotted, know I'm a soft touch."

He got out then to load in a lady and her luggage, and sure enough, the bearded fellow in the baggy, ill-matched coat and trousers came shuffling across the street between cars and cabs and small business vans to get his daily handout.

"He won't hit me up anymore today, though," said my driver friend, climbing back in the limo.

"Do you know anything about him? Where he came from or anything?" I asked.

"He tells a weird tale about himself. Says he was in a concentration camp in Germany when the war was ending. And they took all the prisoners out and put them in a ditch and machine-gunned them. He was covered by a bunch of other bodies and none of the bullets hit 'im. Said he saw that as a sign that he was a favored son of God. So he came over here after the war and never worked another day. So . . . I dunno. Maybe he is.

"I tell ya, I know what it is to be down and out. One time back in the thirties, I was workin' in New York and I didn't have enough to rent a room. For a nickel you could get a ride on the subway, so I'd get on the subway, stretch out on the benches to sleep, and ride all night. Then in the morning I'd get off at my stop and go to work. Did that for about a week and a half till I got enough money for a room. Nobody paid no attention to ya. Wasn't bad. The benches was different then. Long and . . ."

". . . hard-woven straw. Right?"

"Yeah, right. They was straw. Not no more."

"Somebody wrote a play called *Subways Are for Sleeping,* but I never understood what they meant until now."

"Is that right?"

"I guess it was really a musical."

"Well, I'll be darned. Whatta ya do for excitement back on the farm in Ohio?" he asked as we pulled up at the air terminal.

"I turn socks and mend overalls and bake bread, help my husband in the field, and do pretty much what other folks do," I said as I paid him and gave him enough of a tip to subsidize one or two of the old fellows on his "payroll."

"Yeah, folks are pretty much the same wherever you go, aren't they."

"Yup, pretty much the same. There's good and there's bad, but the best ones are crisp on the outside and soft in the middle," I said, giving him a wink and saying goodbye.

Winter

Though winter wraps us in her white scarves deeply,
And the stiff wind sings of owls and wolves,
And the snow thickens, thickens,
We are kept civilized
By the smell of new bread . . .

—Mary Oliver, "Winter at Bellside"

Sneak Play

It was a Christmas party calling for something "smashing." Everything in my closet seemed lackluster. I conjured a vision of Cinderella Leimbach sweeping into the ball in an elegant something from Von Furstenburg or Nina Ricci. Realism told me it was going to be a Leimbach from Singer if anything. Velvet maybe, blue velvet. . . .

I never lost the vision nor found the time, but the morning of the party, out doing errands, I said to myself (as I have too often said to myself), "Why not?" There is no power like unto that of a woman with a vision of herself in some special new finery. I was twenty congested miles from the kitchen where I was due in half an hour to make it seem that lunch was happening.

I whipped into a parking space, tore into the fabric shop, and flipped through a pattern book. "Make it today, wear it tonight," a caption jumped out at me. ALL-RIGHT! I chose some blue velveteen, located the pattern in the big steel file drawer, matched the thread, paid, and left.

After a tardy lunch I stretched out the velveteen, pinned the pattern, and cut out a jumper, eliminating the cautious deliberations usually invested in such a project. At 2:30 Paul interrupted to send me to town for a fan belt. I was loathe to tell him I was up to the old mischief, so I went without protest.

At 4:00 I threaded the sewing machine, set up the ironing board, and filled the steam iron. The party was scheduled for 7:00. Paul, in from his day's work, settled down with the Denver Broncos and the Pittsburgh Steelers while I sewed frantically. Long years of this folly have taught me to keep it low-key. He paid no attention to my project, and I said nothing.

About 6:00 he called from his seat on the fifty-yard line, "Better start thinking of getting ready, Hon." As casually as possible I said, "I just have to finish this hem." It was an exaggeration to say the least. I was still attaching the straps and had a facing to sew on.

"What! Are you making a dress? H ___ !" he muttered, and then the old cliché, "You've got a whole closetful of dresses up there. What's the matter with them?" A rhetorical question if ever there was one.

"But it's a holiday. I need something festive."

"Did I get a 'festive' new suit?"

"That's different."

"No, it isn't different. I'll never understand women!"

He settled low in his chair in a familiar sulk. How many times in thirty years had we played this scene to its explosive conclusion? A hundred? Big evening, last-minute push. Pat in a nervous sweat at the sewing machine, Paul building a head of steam, waiting. All those dozens of hand-sewn dresses through the years, not a leisurely hem in the lot of them.

Asking for help to pin a hem at 6:30 was to wave a red flag before a bull, but I slipped on the jumper and timidly solicited an opinion on length.

"Too _____ long," he grumbled.

"How much shorter?"

"Three inches," he muttered.

Rushing around in my underwear, I eyeballed the hemline, estimating three inches. No time for hand sewing. If the stitch witchery worked, I was home free. If not, it was back to the closet and pick some tired garment from a bygone holiday, bright visions of being a sensation in blue velveteen fading into oblivion.

It was nearly 7:00 and he hadn't budged from his chair to dress. The sulk was very deep, eruption very near. . . .

"Ten seconds!" he yelled. "Fourth down and one yard for a touchdown!" He had forgotten me and the dress and the party and his sulk. The Denver Broncos were staging a coup on the Pittsburgh Steelers. "If they pull this off, it'll be a real upset!"

God bless the Denver Broncos! They didn't bring it off, but I did —gained one yard of blue velveteen hem. By the time he remembered that he was angry with me, I was buttoning my coat over the blue velveteen. First time I've scored in this game in thirty years.

"The Stars Are Brightly Shining"

A poetic fire flickers on the hearth, a couple of fragrant candles glow, and a red poinsettia lends a glory to the room. Paul and the boys have stretched and yawned, looked to the morrow, and gone to bed. I sit alone in the lamplight, as in many a Christmas week of yore, working some gift embroidery.

A piece of needlework is as much a work of fantasy as it is of art or craftsmanship. But take this vacant chair, put your feet on the hassock here with mine, and I'll share some of the musing sewn into this linen along with the blue floss. It is to appearances a tiny church flanked by evergreens in relief against a night sky. The clock on the church tower says midnight. The sky is studded with stars . . . stars in the mind's eye of the embroideress. In her reverie this is a tapestry woven with the bright and varied threads of Christmases past.

There she is at five or six, already excited at the shape of a doll box. This one reveals a baby doll with a cloth body and pink plaster head, hands, and feet. Later there would be dolls of rubber, dolls that opened and closed their eyes and cried and wet their diapers, dolls with painted hearts, and stiffly beautiful Shirley Temple dolls with frilly dresses and shiny hair, pretty to look at, disappointing to hold.

There's our Christmas tree in '47—nearly perfect. Brother Bill "made" it himself. It was the last one Frankie Linn had on the lot, tall and spindly with great spaces between branches. The price was right, so Bill dragged it home, sawed it apart, and spliced it together with lengths of pipe. So splendid! Decorated with those snow-covered cottages, lights shining through tiny cellophane windows, and that peculiar star Mary bought during the war with her hard-earned money.

She held three jobs at once as a college student and still found time to make nearly all her Christmas gifts. One year there was a woolen scarf threaded with yarn fringe; another year, an orange pomander ball that left a permanent scent of spice in the china cabinet.

Mother is a potent spirit hovering about this tapestry. All alone she seemed to make Christmas happen. Daddy didn't keep Christmas. Only once did he buy a gift, had Mary choose a nightie for Mama. He died two weeks later, and she never wore it, just folded it away in tissue paper in her bottom drawer. We would peek at it sometimes when she was out, show our friends and whisper, "This is the nightie Daddy gave Mama . . ."

Here we are in the kitchen, Mama and I, when I was older and trying to master the old family cooking secrets, making plum pudding, cutting suet into tiny pieces, working in the figs and dates with our hands. Such awful stuff to emerge from the steamer tasting so good as the climax of the feast—dark and rich and fruity, served on the glass plates, with lemon sauce.

And my older brothers here, coming in sheepishly on Christmas Eve with great boxes of lacy things, asking, "Do you suppose you could wrap this for Alice? . . . for Mabel? . . . for Gerri?"

Woven into this corner, the Christmas dance of my college dreams —my junior year, at the Hotel Cleveland with my Prince Charming of that year. Just smashing I was, in my green velvet strapless, the sewing project of one entire December, and the African kidskin coat brother John had lavished upon me. John was there too with my little college roommate. We drank our first champagne that night from a silver loving cup. Oh my! Christmas itself was an anticlimax.

Here's the honeymoon Christmas in Florida, a red flannel nightgown for a gift, both of us a little blue spending our first Christmas away from home, but not admitting it.

And from then on there were little boys at Christmas—one, then two, then three—and drums and trains, sleds and ice skates, tractors and popguns. Little boys lighting Advent candles, being angels and wise men, struggling with scripture, trying to make sense of the Christmas story.

Here's little Jeffrey the year his mother died, coming to live with us, introducing Dane to Christmas stockings late Christmas Eve. "If ya hang your socks up, Dane, Santa leaves stuff in 'em." Somewhere Santa found small things to fill them.

Santa Claus! Of course he's there, in bright red flannel and full beard. This one looks ever so slightly like Uncle Hank. Why, it is Hank! . . . up in the toy department at Western Auto, and the nephews cuddled on his lap are none the wiser.

So many years of sewing and wrapping all night, crawling into bed at gray dawn as the boys awoke. So many years in the lamplight of midnight, sewing. . . .

Above the little church I outline one final star, bigger and brighter than the others, the eternal Star of Bethlehem—the star on the tree, the star in the eyes, the glow in the heart, the Hope of the World—golden threads in a Christmas tapestry.

Coming to Terms

Taking inventory on the thirteenth day of Christmas I find that I still have a few needs beyond a partridge in a pear tree. Nothing major, but a lot of little nagging things: a new dishcloth, washers on my faucets, a new broom, a belt for my vacuum cleaner, a pedal for my bike, a ribbon for my typewriter, shoelaces, a toothbrush, a new toilet plunger, tags for my dogs, clean paper on the kitchen shelves.

None of these items, or the lack of them, is really causing me distress. When worse comes to worst, my needs will be met. It's what I've got that I don't need that's distressing me. A new year! Who needs a new year? If you ran the old one past me again, I still wouldn't be finished with it. I figure I'm presently working on mid-1975, though in truth, there's stuff here plaguing me that dates back to the fifties.

There's an antique tie quilt up in the linen closet that I've been going to finish mending since '52, a sampler I started for my mother in '59, and a quilt top of hers I never got into the quilt frames. Now my mother is dead and gone, and the projects remain to haunt me. In fact, there is much about my mother's life that haunts me—her effects, those boxes, bags, drawers, closets, attics full of all the things she was one day going to do, things she hoped to sort over, reread, appraise, and organize. She slipped away from it all long before she died, but somewhere in her being was the lingering frustration.

Another year . . . Inevitable. Perhaps I should make a few resolutions I really intend to follow:

Be it here resolved that I will never mend that tie quilt or finish that sampler. I will never reread my old love letters, never stick all those photos into little gummed corners and arrange them in albums with captions (for myself or the kids), nor will I assemble that great mass of clippings, book reviews, cartoons, programs, and gilt-edged certificates into neatly labeled scrapbooks.

Let it be further resolved that I will never refinish that swivel chair in the cellar, reupholster the love seat, make a slipcover for the chaise lounge on the porch, or create embroidered coverlets from my collection of little boys' drawings; moreover, I will never braid rugs out of all those woolens in the attic, nor will I sort and recopy my recipe collection. Never will I reread all those *National Geographics*, iron and utilize the used gift wrap, frame that collection of *New Yorker* covers, knit afghans from the bag of yarn scraps. I will never create formal gardens on the side hill or have a rose arbor to interest *Better Homes and Gardens*.

Be it resolved, finally, that like my mother before me, I will do, day to day, the things that life demands and rejoice in that accomplishment.

Anatomy of an Obsession

I've been back three times to look at the coat, like a child with a fixation for some toy in a store window. This coat is about as lovely as the rear quarters of an elephant and almost the same color, and it's just what I want.

"Who in the Sam Hill will ever buy this?" I asked the clerk when I first tried it on.

"We sold one to a lady whose husband was transferred to Alaska. She was delighted. They'd be great for football games."

"Or if you were standing the night watch on the Murmansk run," I said, pulling up the shawl collar, buttoning it around my face, and turning to get the back view. It hung to my ankles. Quite a sight. A couple of other clerks stopped to kibitz.

"The way I see it, you've got two options with that coat. You can sew it together at the top and make a tent, or you can seam it at the bottom and make a sleeping bag."

Still . . . there was something about it that appealed to me. It was snug and cozy and light as a feather pillow despite the bulky quilting. If I had to lug it around when I was traveling, chuck it up into an airplane compartment, or pull it over me as I slept on a bench, it would be great. I'd better get Paul's opinion.

Maybe subconsciously I just wanted to create a controversy. I knew darned well what Paul's opinion was going to be.

"You aren't going to wear that coat when you're with me!" he said vehemently.

"But honey, it's so warm and so light and so practical."

"Practical, baloney! It's so long you can't walk in it, and the pockets hit you right at the knees." With that he set his jaw. It is at this precise moment that woman knows she cannot live without the object that man is disputing. I took up the gauntlet.

The clerk was trying to mollify him. She got down on her knees and folded under a foot of hem.

"If you could just envision it shorter, you'd see that it's really rather attractive. It's a marvelous buy, a wonderful piece of fabric."

"She looks like she just escaped from Siberia."

"This is a very fashionable look," I said. There was blood in his eye. He was in no mood for haute couture.

"I'm telling you again, I won't be seen with you in that coat!" The clerk scurried away to avoid a confrontation.

"Honey," I whispered, "it's a terrific buy. It was $130, marked down to $65!"

"The clerk is probably getting 50 percent of that for moving it out of here," he grumbled.

I continued to study myself in the mirror, buttoning and unbuttoning, cocking my head to one side insouciantly—a Cheryl Tieg, tall and lovely, lending style to everything I gathered to my body.

I was Pat Leimbach, short and dumpy, looking like a refugee. It was awful.

"I don't know why you ask for my opinion," said Paul. "You made up your mind before you ever brought me here." He wasn't getting the vision. We left.

But I can't forget it. If only he'd said, "Terrific! It's you!" I would have backed off immediately.

The decision dominated my week. I saw myself everywhere in that coat—going out to the mailbox on blustery days, hopping into a cold pickup truck to get some lady a bag of potatoes, getting on and off little commuter planes, caught in a blizzard, trudging through drifts—warm and secure, my Murmansk collar around my ears. It saves my life. Paul is glad I have it.

A third time I went to look at it, hoping secretly that it would be gone, bought by somebody moving to International Falls, Minnesota, or the girlfriend of a linebacker for the Green Bay Packers. It hung there yet, warm and seductive. I left it behind.

What a petty issue to obsess one. It didn't matter that the government had fallen in another banana republic, or that the Western alliance was threatened, that in many parts of the world people were fleeing from chaos with nothing but the clothes on their backs . . . the clothes on their backs! I know that if I had just one garment in the world to shield me from peril and destruction . . . *that* coat. . . .

Twenty-Twenty Hindsight

My friends Donna and Lobell Bennett thought we should spend the night up in Lewistown. (I was giving a speech there and they had agreed to chauffeur me.) The pleasure they took in the notion was thinly disguised. Somebody had reserved rooms for the three of us in a comfortable establishment there, and it would be a nice change to have a night out, breakfast at the hotel, and a leisurely drive back to Billings in the Montana morning sun. Yes, they relished the notion.

It was, they pointed out, a drive of 160 miles through wild and woolly territory. Ranches would be few and far between, and the snow accumulation this winter was extraordinary—they hadn't seen the ground since November. In truth, only a fool would consider driving that wilderness on a February night.

I'd just survived a string of twelve or fourteen nights in motels with their cold, impersonal appointments. I had a 7:00 a.m. plane out of Billings, and I couldn't catch it lounging about till late morning in a motel 160 miles away.

The road looked straight and flat on the map. We were driving up in the afternoon, and surely if conditions were so bad as to caution against our late night return, we would know it by the time we got to Lewistown. In an emergency we could take a motel in Grassrange or Roundup, the two towns that lay along the route.

A call in the morning from the folks up in Lewistown was thoroughly pessimistic. Were we coming? The roads beyond Lewistown were impassable to Great Falls.

"Of course we're coming," I said. "I haven't flown from Texas to Billings to be deterred by a few drifts." Lobell called the highway department, who were cautious in their affirmation that yes, the roads to Lewistown were open—one lane in a few places, and blowing snow, but . . .

All that was wanted, I was convinced, was positive thinking. It had been a humdinger of a winter, and I was already a veteran of these tough driving campaigns.

Donna began assembling gear—three big garbage sacks containing sleeping bags! Sleeping bags? "Oh, yes," she said matter-of-factly. "We wouldn't dream of traveling these plains at night without protection against exposure." They put in their suitcases (just in case), a bag of food, a shovel, boots, and heaven knows what other survival equipment, and we took off.

Just as I had supposed, the roads were clear and in most places dry. Here and there a drift across the road was wet and slushy, but nowhere impassable. The fears planted by those sleeping bags melted with the slush. Lovely drive through . . . well . . . some pretty rugged and forlorn country, far more so than Rand McNally would have you believe. Here and there the snow stood higher than the car on either shoulder.

We found the Eagles Hall and met the local ranchers. ("Local" included everybody within a hundred-mile radius, nearly all planning to pass the night in Lewistown, I discovered to my dis-ease.) We ate and regaled ourselves, the Country Wife gave a rousing speech, and we put on our coats to leave.

"You're not going back to Billings tonight!" folks said with wonder and caution in their tones. "It's snowing blue blazes out there."

Were we home on the range, where seldom is heard a discouraging word? One must not be deterred by timid souls. One other brave fellow 'lowed as how he was fixin' to drive back to Roundup that night.

"Whatta ya drivin'?" asked another.

"A Chevy station wagon," he said.

The Bennetts, bless them, lacked enthusiasm, but they knew I was determined, and they were good sports. The snow seemed innocuous enough falling beneath the streetlights. We got out of town and the white stuff descended like a curtain—"snowing blue blazes."

Should we turn back, admit defeat? I sat tensely in the rear seat, "steering" all the way. Pride and Determination are poor companions in a back seat in the Montana wilds in a snowstorm. I was weakening. At the same time I recognized that Pride and Determination were riding in the front seat with my friends. If I was weakening, their lifetime in this wilderness had prepared them to endure.

Lobell drove on and on through the dense and blowing snow, slowly, persistently. A few trucks came toward us, but no other fools were bound in our direction for Billings. We covered the thirty-one arduous miles to Grassrange. A motel in Grassrange, perhaps? Ha! Grassrange was a scattered cluster of lights off to the right, about as big on the landscape as on the map.

We turned south there, and the wind that had been behind us blew

swirls of snow across our path. The car spun on the slippery pave-
ment. Lobell brought it back under control but too late: we had lost
traction at the foot of a long hill. Donna and I hopped out to push.
We could scarcely get a foothold on the ice, but inch by inch the tires
spun us forward. Like an ace in the hole, I clung to the thought of
that other native coming this route in his Chevy station wagon.

Lights appeared in the distance, proceeded up, and around, and
beyond us—a green Chevy station wagon. Darkness again. Lobell's
car got off on the berm finally and climbed the hill. We ran after,
hopped in, and continued toward Roundup. My only small comfort
was the thought of those sleeping bags.

We kept up a nervous conversation, avoiding mention of the fool-
hardy predicament I had plunged us into, and watched the road
markers tick off the miles. Each of us "drove" the whole nerve-
wracking distance. In Roundup at last the snow subsided; the worst
was over, and we stopped for coffee at an all-night café. I assumed a
"didn't I tell you?" demeanor, but into my coffee I dunked a tough
hunk of crow.

Centennial House

"When I was in the hardware yesterday I noticed they carry those
one-piece shower stalls. Get your rule and let's see if we could fit one
through the southeast window. . . ."

By golly, we could! And that was two weeks, eight trips to town,
ten sheets of drywall, three sheets of plywood, five gallons of paint,
thirty-three feet of plumbing, a roll of wallpaper, nine hundred dollars, and thirty-seven arguments ago.

This dear old house, from a simple beginning with five rooms and
a path (delicately bordered by hollyhocks), at age 125 has swelled to
eight rooms, two baths, a screened-in porch, and an attached garage.
The cellar is vintage 1861.

If a house had a log, like a ship or an airplane, what a tale it could
tell. Some of the saga unfolds as you work on a house, tearing off
plaster, raising a roof, replacing a sill, constructing a dormer, install-
ing a chimney.

Ours gives evidence of having been built in four stages, as a family
grew and funds became available. It was never a rich man's house.

The ceilings were not high and the roof crowded the upstairs bed-rooms. There were no ornate fireplaces and no carved woodwork. Mean little stoves were vented into wall chimneys. The floors were of soft cottonwood, though the structural beams were hand-hewn oak.

There was, however, a chilly little parlor and a proud staircase that opened into a narrow hallway. "Plumbing" was limited to a pitcher pump in the kitchen and a slop jar under each bed.

A gas well drilled early in the century brought gas lights and little gas heaters and a pervasive odor that creeps back whenever the house is empty long. The iron ceiling fixtures with their oil lamps were relegated to the woodshed. Linoleum replaced rag rugs on the worn floors, the small-paned windows were supplanted by large "modern" ones that were easier to clean, the shutters were banished to the barns. The roof was shingled three times over, a gasoline-powered washer appeared in the woodshed, and an extravagant coal-fired hot water boiler was installed.

Paul's grandparents lived in the house when we were married. Paul was the third son in the fourth generation on the farm and he didn't marry young, so his mother had many years to remodel this house in her mind before I came into the picture. I remember that the after-noon we became engaged, she swept through the house sharing vi-sions of raising the roof, tearing down partitions, wiring, plumbing, plastering, papering, all in a joyous outpouring. I was confused by the plan, but she eventually accomplished it all.

Softwood was out, hardwood was in; linoleum was out, carpet was in; parlors were out, living rooms were in; and the house became, as it usually had been in an earlier time, a two-family house. We had the standard "six rooms and bath." Grandpa and Grandma had the side wing.

There have been two or three partial remodelings since. Paul's grandparents died, the woodshed became a garage, the grape arbor became a porch, and the shutters are back, as are the iron ceiling lamps, wired for electricity this time. The "sitting room" became a family room with kitchen, and my tiny old kitchen is at long last Paul's office, with a little downstairs bath like every young mother dreams of and nobody who's fifty needs at all. What I really wanted in there (to the loud objection of my men) was a laun-dry, which would have gotten me up out of that cold, dim, damp, dirty cellar.

"Well," says Paul smugly as he's cleaning his painting tools, "we have now redone every darned room in this house. This should hold us for the rest of our lives."

HO! HO! HO! There's a Russian proverb that says, "When the house is finished, the man dies."

A washer and drier might just fit into that upstairs bathroom if we would tear out . . .

Cost Accounting

"Have you thought about what you want for curtains in this bathroom?" said Paul, standing back and surveying his accomplishments with the unique satisfaction of a do-it-yourselfer.

"No, I haven't," I said, realizing that it was a fib. What woman ever plans a room without hanging the curtains long in advance in the windows of her imagination? She may not admit it to herself, but there is a dream, however elusive it may be.

The bathroom curtains of my fancy are of white embroidered eyelet like those I saw hanging one winter long ago in the tiny Dutch homes of the storybook village of Vollendam on the Zuider Zee. They spoke of purity and order and tradition and, I suppose, of fairy tales. I had thought about those curtains for twenty-five years, had hung them in spirit in every room I'd decorated since. But always there was some economic compromise, and I chose other curtains instead.

On a damp country morning when Paul was out delivering potatoes, he willingly dropped me off at the fabric shop to choose curtain material. One thing we were agreed upon: a room isn't done until the curtains are up.

It didn't take me long to eliminate a hundred bolts of white fabric. There was only one I really wanted, the most expensive fabric in the shop. There were a couple of others that would do in a pinch—the sort I'd settled on all my life.

But there was only one small window. . . . Why not? I'll pay for them, and Paul need never know what they cost. He'll just assume I made a good buy.

"Four yards," I said to the clerk, pushing the bolt toward her. Inside me reason and desire were locked in a death struggle. "Thirty-two dollars for one curtain? That doesn't even allow for tiebacks or labor. You're out of your mind! That other stuff hasn't as much body, but who'll know the difference?

"I'll know, that's who! What's thirty-two dollars? Two sacks of groceries. Eat 'em up in a few days, and what have you got to show for it? The curtains will be hanging there for years, each day a joy. Think how long you've wanted them. . . . Go ahead. . . . You're not going to live forever!"

Desire had a stranglehold on reason. It was too late to back out. Those wide-whacking shears had cut clean through that width of neat white eyelet.

I unsnapped my wallet. Empty!

The rest was predictable. Paul returned, and I asked him for thirty-two dollars.

"Thirty-two dollars! For one lousy curtain? That's twelve bags of potatoes!" Paul had been hanging curtains in his mind, too. He remembers them from the Sears Roebuck catalog of his youth, flouncy things in a choice of white or pastel shades: "Good quality, $2.98; better quality, $3.98; best quality, $4.98."

We drove home in silence, I clutching the small sack of dream stuff, feeling like a child caught shoplifting; Paul, his jaw set in that firm disapproving line, weighing the bulk of twelve bags of potatoes against that small white sack on my lap.

The curtain is hung, and it's lovely. The tiebacks are fashioned from scraps of green velveteen. The white eyelet embroidery speaks softly of wood shoes, shining windows, and sails on the Zuider Zee. The family is eating a lot of potatoes, and thirty-two dollars doesn't seem a bad price for an enduring Dutch reverie.

Roots

I once published an essay alluding to "the Heinzerling eyes," a family feature I hear mentioned at Leimbach reunions. As a result there came to me a letter from one Pauline Burgdorf in southern Indiana asking about the possibility of our origination from the same Heinzerling stem somewhere. In view of the fact that the Heinzerlings were my husband's kinfolk, I turned the letter over to an aunt of his, who passed it on to another, who gave it to a cousin, who corresponded with Pauline, and together they ironed out this weighty matter.

One recent winter I was down in the Evansville, Indiana, area speaking for a soil conservation meeting, and who should surface again but Pauline Burgdorf, come around to see if I have the Heinzerling eyes. My eyes came down to me from the lady-in-waiting to one of the beheaded wives of Henry the Eighth and a mixed bag of English bishops, rogues, and scalawags, but I didn't tell Pauline.

We made arrangements to meet, and the next day she came in her little red Volkswagen. I wedged myself and my luggage in with Mama Luise Burgdorf, a box of books, and bags of Heinzerling keepsakes, and we bounced off across Posey County, Indiana, in search of the ghosts of our common ancestors.

We did a couple of cemeteries, an assortment of churches, and a spate of old farmhouses in varying stages of deterioration. We crept in low gear down to the flooded banks of the Ohio River to the tiny and now defunct community where the Heinzerlings and the Beckers (whom they married) once disembarked from their longboats or their birchbark canoes or their rafts—who knows?—and staked out their claim on a section or two of scenic woodland.

Over lunch we pored through genealogies and photographs and *alte deutsche Bücher* while Pauline shared with me her quest for her roots, reading tombstones, church registries, courthouse records, and faded letters. She shared with me, too, the rich fulfillment of her quest, memories and mementos of her trips to visit her contemporary cousins in Hessen and Westfalen in northern Germany.

Pauline Burgdorf is not your ordinary, now-and-then collector of ancestral relics. Among the memorabilia she has acquired to keep her mindful of who she is and where she came from is a church founded by the congregation of which her forebears were a part. When a new church was built on the original site in 1973 and the little white frame church with the tin steeple and the red, white, and blue stained glass windows was threatened with destruction, Pauline bought it. She paid $5,000 to have it moved to a new location three miles away. Her hope is to restore it to its original beauty.

In the late afternoon we followed a gravel road up into the wooded hills, parked, and trudged along a trail to the site of the original dwelling built by the Heinzerlings in the Posey County wilderness 140 years ago. As the sun was setting, Pauline drove me back to the cemetery where stands the tombstone she designed and had cut for her own parents. On it, carved in old German script, are the verses from their confirmation certificates.

I was bemused by this one woman's determined quest for her origins. There was something poignant in watching her there in the woods by the leaf-covered dimple in the ground where that original cabin had stood. To Pauline it was as real as if she had hewed the logs for the roof beam. Hers was an enviable zeal. I was pleased that she had involved me in her discoveries. I didn't tell her, of course, but Pauline didn't have the Heinzerling eyes.

Ex Libris!

"What do you mean, 'get rid of some of those books!'? Writers don't throw books away. They collect books. What we need to do is extend those shelves to the ceiling."

"Well, I'm not building any more bookshelves. You've got double rows of books on three of those shelves. Now you figure out what you're going to do with them."

"But I refer to those books all the time. Most of them are classics."

"When was the last time you delved into that old classic *Beginning French*? You haven't opened any of those language books in thirty years."

"Well, what about all your German lit books? They've been there just as long as my French books. And we could save half a shelf if we'd get rid of those Ohio State yearbooks. We haven't used them since the kids were big enough to reach the table without sitting on books."

"What about *your* college yearbooks with all those pictures of the 'jolly girls' in them?"

I could see that we were getting into dangerous territory. I dropped the discussion and went about sorting books. So many good old "friends" here, books I read in the confusion of young womanhood with a woeful ignorance of what life was all about—novels by Stendhal and Pasternak, Dostoyevsky and Victor Hugo, books to be re-read in the wisdom of age looking back nostalgically at that naive young woman. You can't throw them away!

And I certainly can't discard the little collection of regional histories given me by farm people around the country, unique tales of the settlers written by somebody's grandmother or the local librarian.

There's a precious clutch of essays by my beloved E. B. White. I can't let *those* go, nor can I part with intimates like Thomas Hardy, George Eliot, the Brontes.

I might get along without one of these sets of youth encyclopedias, but then, we'll have grandchildren coming along. . . . *The Rise and Fall of the Third Reich* takes a lot of space. I never did get through that, but I really should one day. . . .

There are Gladys Taber's *Stillmeadow* books. They tided Mama through a lot of difficult years. Think she always dreamed I'd grow up to be Gladys Taber. I must keep them a while longer. It's too soon . . .

There are other books here made precious by an inscription from Mama—*Bullfinch's Mythology, Biographies of Famous Women, The Poems of Longfellow.* (I'm glad she never knew that Longfellow was castigated by later critics.)

And all the literary anthologies stuffed with clippings about authors —they certainly deserve a shelf of their own, along with the poetry. I suppose I could part with *Laundered Limericks.*

Fanny Hill! The book that taught everyone the meaning of "unexpurgated." Now there's a classic. And those McGuffey Readers— better get them on a different shelf from *Fanny Hill.* Here's a collector's item, a book called *Adolf Hitler* given to us by a German cousin who was bombed out twice during the war. Somehow the book survived. As premiums for cigarette wrappers, she said, people were given photographs to paste into these propaganda books. Most of them made great bonfire material after the war. I'll put it back on the wide lower shelf alongside *Wilhelm Busch, The Progress of the Protestant,* the high school yearbooks, and that stack of Ohio State Makios.

Yes, we compromised; we kept his, and we kept mine—all sixteen of them, representing six institutions of learning and a lot of forgotten friends. We kept the German literature and the French grammars, too, and a couple hundred novels alphabetized from Agee to Wouk, from Balzac to Vonnegut. I dusted and reshelved all the old college textbooks of science, knowing full well that nobody would ever read again *Bacterial and Mycotic Infections of Man,* but . . .

Paul brought a big box for the discards, but it wasn't collecting much. I made a little stack of other people's books to return and a second stack to go to the church library. I ran through the tomes on social and religious issues: the black movement, the God-is-dead movement, the sensitivity movement, zen and mysticism, abortion —permanent states of confusion all. Nothing expendable here.

Listen, Yankee, C. Wright Mills's book about the Cuban revolution written in 1960—there's a dead issue if there ever was one. I dropped it into the box, and then an impulse born of a warm memory caused me to retrieve it and open the brittle browning pages.

In the winter of 1956 C. Wright Mills and I spent a carefree afternoon in Munich visiting the Haus der Kunst, shopping at Loden-Frey, stopping for warmth and beer at the Hofbrau Haus. I didn't know him from Adam, only that he was a writer and a bon vivant and rode a BMW motorcycle. (We were accidental participants in a motorcycle dealers' tour to Germany.) Now he's dead and gone and I think of all the erudite questions I might have asked.

I slumped there behind the couch and became engrossed in the Cuban revolution and C. Wright Mills's predictions of dominolike revolutions throughout the "hungry nations" of the world. A dead issue? Certainly not. Rather, a "history written in advance" of an ongoing movement. I put it back on the shelf.

It's no use, Paul. Somebody else will have to dispose of these books when I'm gone, someone whose life is not so intertwined with all they contain.

The Winter of '78

Every conversation (over the phone, at the kitchen door, across the meat counter, after church) is weighted heavily with winter. People are eager for sassafras and pussy willows, hungry for green and the rustles of spring. I feel like the lone subversive.

Every morning that I look out and see the drifts still high and plump, I rejoice. I like the way they flow over the fences and hide the cars from view. I like walking three feet above the backyard to dump my garbage behind the kettle house. Paul has had to dig the firewood from a snowbank and push coal to the coal chute in the wheelbarrow because neither truck nor wagon could get near. That seems a delightful fact to record for posterity. Icicles hang from the roof to the ground of the seed house. Rabbits have stood on drifts and chewed the bark from the fire thorn and denuded all the lower limbs of the euonymus. The footpaths and the roadways to the barns are deep ditches cut through the snow, and I don't want to part with any of it!

This winter has been the fulfillment of my every childhood dream of what winter should be, the way no Ohio winter ever really was before or probably ever will be again.

Oh, the snow has come each winter, piled in spectacular drifts. For a day or two we were drawn together as this year in satisfying isolation. But then a warming trend, a thaw, and it was spent in ugliness. The white mass was at last overcome by the salt and the road crews. But the best efforts of all of us have not defeated winter this year.

Like everyone else, I have been inconvenienced. Since the snow fell on January 1, I have been back and forth to Iowa, Indiana, Illinois, Michigan, Montana, Minnesota, Pennsylvania, North Dakota, Kentucky, and the Carolinas. I have been at times cold, tired, frightened, ill, and frustrated, yet I have not had my fill of this amazing winter.

With the exuberance of New Year's Eve, Teddy and his friends fired off a couple of packs of firecrackers out front. The porch and the yard were littered with fitzels of Chinese newspaper, and Ted's parents delivered a lecture on responsibility. "I'll rake it all up in the morning," he insisted, and we let him off with that promise.

The debris from all those firecrackers is still out there under the snow, along with the twigs and dead branches blown down in the January blizzard. There's a tractor muffler buried somewhere, along with pans and bowls set out with dog scraps. There are the usual tin cans and bones and lost gloves—all that to come to light before the crocuses, all of that to skim from the mud. For who is so naive as to think we shall not have mud time to rival the record snows?

I am content to sit by the fire a while longer and spin a long yarn to relate in the dim future to my grandchildren. ". . . And would you believe that the rabbits could stand on the snowdrifts and eat the bark right off the branches of the pear tree?"

"Awww . . . Grammaw!"

Diaspora

This is the week of the move, and I am not resigned. Dane talks of the logistics: "We'll have four vehicles with the van, so it'll mean two trips." Karen has the entryway stacked with boxes, each filled by reluctant hands. Kelly doesn't want to leave her friends, the new bedroom is "too small," and there's no safe place for the cat.

Karen's mother is on the phone sharing her desolation: "I have six other kids to fret over, and I'm still just sick about their moving." But they're going, our son, his wife, and his stepdaughter.

Grand Rapids, Michigan, isn't the end of the world, but it's too far to phone and say, "Why not come out for supper?" or, "We'll be away. Could you stop by the farm and check on things?" Orrin won't have his big brother to run to with technological problems. No more early evening footsteps on the porch presaging a cheery, impromptu visit, Dane prowling about the house checking the mail and the magazines, searching for the little signs that have measured the passage of life in his absence.

This is dreadful! And it happens all the time in everybody's family. Americans are inveterate nomads. What is the statistic? One family in four moves every year? Why not rise in protest of all this upheaval?

Yes, it happens in everybody's family, but not in mine. I live ten miles from the house where I was born and grew up, and for many years I was the farthest from home of my mother's seven children. All my brothers built houses on the farm and stayed there. Our children grew up together as we had, a happy tribe. Christmas and Easter, Halloween and the Fourth of July, Thanksgiving and New Year's, and on everybody's birthday at least part of the clan gathered —still gathers. When Erik and Alice announced several years back that they were buying a farm forty miles south, we were all aghast. How would they survive down there alone? They did survive, of course, but we burn a lot of gas maintaining this outpost down in Polk.

Now our families have grown, each with initial solidarity, then little by little torn by the societal forces that prevail in the nation. The opportunities, the amenities, the action is elsewhere, so the young people go. The sun and the mountain breezes comfort the frail of limb and the thin of blood, so the grandparents go. Too many islands cut off from the mainland.

Cousins grow up not knowing cousins, not caring, moreover. What you do, how you live is of little consequence to the new neighbors, the new community. They didn't know your parents or your grandparents, after all. The relatives at a distance are out of touch. Ties are broken. Old prohibitions often fall away.

Our sons have a strange affinity for this paradise of their childhood, this End o' Way, this home of their forefathers. Unlike other children, they never chafed to get away. They have gone often, and happily, for the brief or extended intervals demanded by their education and their avocations. And they have seen other Edens, but home lies cradled in an ample bend of the Vermilion River between Swift's Hollow and Schmalz's flats.

Dane had a spot picked out on the bank up by the Indian fort where he was planning to dig a well next spring and build his dream castle. Karen came out in the fall to help with the potato harvest and had begun to think she might like to farm someday with her brother-in-law. Kelly suspected that one of those old barns could be remodeled to suit a horse.

No, they never planned to move to Grand Rapids. But that is suddenly where the job has moved, so they're packing boxes. Something in me wants to believe that they'll be back, but "knowing how way leads on to way, . . ." Well, I am not resigned.

Transplantation

My friends Dot and Henry Schriver are paramount among the folks farmers look to for leadership in our county. Their tribe of eleven have spread themselves all across America, and most of them are involved somehow in agriculture. In the course of my travels I often find myself in Schriver territory, where the latchstring is always out.

I once spent an hour or two on a hot, dry August afternoon looking for Bill Schriver's farm out in east-central Nebraska. "Oh sure, we know Bill's place. You go five squares that way, three squares north, and then two west. Sets on a hillside. You can't miss it. . . ." But I did. My time ran out and I drove on, wondering what Bill's place would have looked like. Several winters later, I found out.

Bill was having breakfast in the Grand Island airport when I arrived for our rendezvous. He was unmistakable—a younger, handsomer version of his dad. Bill had learned I was in Nebraska and volunteered to fly me out along the Platte to keep a speaking appointment. He had a little Cessna Starfire at the time, which he owned with four other Cornhuskers.

We took off in the clear, still morning and flew toward Gothenburg, a hundred miles westward. Beneath us the South Platte ("a mile wide and an inch deep") spread out on the plain, a broad, irregular braid of intertwining streams. A flock of sandhill cranes in early migration glided in to feed among the sheltering islands.

Bill handed me the map, entrusting me with the responsibility for visual navigation. "That's Kearney down there," he said. "See the airstrip?"

"Uh huh," I said, but I wasn't seeing it. He was asking about radio numbers, elevations, obstructions—all inscribed on the map—and I tried to gloss over my ignorance of aeronautical terms and references.

"Well, if that's Kearney, that must be Odessa down there, and that must be Elm Creek. Yup, there comes the highway down from the north." I was unnerved at locating highways without numbers, but having certified Elm Creek I was gaining confidence. I scanned the prairies, searching for the little towns. There were Overton and Lexington . . . Darr, and Cozad . . . and Gothenburg! This time I could find the airstrip east of town. Bill contacted somebody hanging around the station there and they "rogered" us in.

A woman met and whisked us off to the local high school, where I was introduced and spoke to 300 farm wives from the local farm cooperative. Then we were ferried back to the airstrip and took off for Omaha.

If I could get there in time I could catch a 5:49 flight for Cleveland and save myself a day's travel. But it was going to be nip and tuck. "Let's forget it and fly home to Albion," I said, but Bill was stimulated by the challenge.

We followed the railroads, the elevators, and the water towers across the prairie and landed in Omaha just as the Cleveland flight was getting takeoff clearance from the tower . . . and up it went like a great gander. Nice try.

Off we flew again, toward Albion this time, by the light of a full moon. We picked out the beacon of the airstrip, and the landing lights winking on automatically as we settled down.

Home, then, in the subzero night to the Schriver haven, a moonlit outpost on a hillside dominated by three silver grain bins. It's a nondescript old farmhouse that Bill and Dee have improved and expanded, made cozy and lived-in. A welcoming fire burned on the hearth of the new family room. (There were a lot of "new farm family rooms" built in the brief affluent flush of the seventies.) A hot supper waited in the comfortable, cluttered kitchen. A new baby girl slept in an infant seat on the counter.

Nine years earlier Bill and Dee had migrated to eastern Nebraska, beginning with nothing but a huge debt at the bank but intent on pursuing the family farm tradition. (It was quite clear that the future for a young grain farmer in our industrial, suburbanized area of northern Ohio was limited.) It wasn't as perilous as starting West in a covered wagon, but there were modern pitfalls every bit as forbidding.

Now they owned 400 acres and rented 800 more, about half of it under pivot irrigation. They had a barnful of tractors and a lotful of equipment. (And twice as much indebtedness, speaking of pitfalls.) They had four little girls and a son who attended a two-room country grade school down the road. They had responsibilities at the church, on the school board, and with the Natural Resources Board and, like the Schrivers of Lorain County, Ohio, a community of friends who valued them highly.

Bill took me back to Omaha in the morning. As we rose above the hangar and the rolling countryside, I said, "Now that it's daylight, Bill, show me your farm," and he pointed it out below.

"Ah, yes, I see. . . . Where the grain bins are."

"That's home," said Bill.

Thimble Therapy

Paul brushed down the cobwebs; I creamed the chicken and swept the porch. Harriet arrived at 8:45 with the needles and put in the first stitches, and our quilting bee was under way. (And high time, too. The quilt had been "up" in the living room for nine weeks.)

A quilting bee is the darndest shindig you ever heard tell of. You invite these talented and energetic women to come and work, and they act as if you'd done them a favor. They'll knot their threads at 9:00 and quit reluctantly at 5:00 when their husbands are on the phone asking, "What's for supper?" And they don't clutter up the day with coffee breaks.

In between there's a constant stream of chatter, most of it on the work in progress, though the quilting bees of yore and the great quilters of yesteryear come in for plenty of comment. A few of the old pros are still among us, and I had several of them sewing fine curlicues for me the winter I finally did Mama's quilt top, the one she'd worked at all through my childhood.

Elsie Schmalz pushes a "hot needle," and Mildred Henning can't sleep nights if she knows there's a friendly quilt unfinished somewhere in the township. She'll pop in on you after the quilting bee, saying, "I just thought I'd finish that row of blocks so we could turn that side." Hazel Northeim is renowned in quilting circles for sewing the evenest stitches. Harriet Wise is our consulting expert. The rest of us enjoy amateur status.

The ground rules for a quilting bee are rather subtly delineated as the morning progresses. (Paul learned them all as a child playing hide-and-seek under the quilt frames at his mother's quilting parties.) Stitches should be tiny and even. "Why don't you ever invite Maggie Kawasaki to your quilting bees? She does a lot of quilting," I once asked my mother-in-law.

"That's not quilting," she snapped. "That's just basting stitches." She set back my quilting twenty-five years with that remark.

Woe be unto her whose stitches do not penetrate the underside! She will be the absent subject of considerable comment at the next quilting bee. The supreme ignominy is having it known that your hostess later ripped out and requilted all you sewed. Aunt Lou Kneisel was cited as the sort of fastidious quilter capable of such effrontery.

If you attempt to quilt without a thimble, you will draw disapproving glances over the tops of veteran spectacles. Any dummy knows, of course, that you sew with the thread in the direction it comes off the spool, knotting the end you most recently cut. And no self-respecting quilter would think of leaving knots visible in her work. There are lots of sidelong glances to see how *your* work stacks up with the rest.

Custom differs on the amount of quilting you should accomplish to merit lunch. In some circles it is suggested you should quilt enough that you could sit on it, which places quite a burden on those ladies with large derrieres. We settled for an area the size of a dinner plate. (There are those at my party who got by on a salad plate, though I won't publish their names.)

Nor will I noise it around that Paul was in there on his knees that night checking the underside of the quilt with a flashlight. I told him that if he planned to rip out any of that stitching, he was on his own. My big concern was with enticing them all back. We had finished forty blocks and had seventy to go. (Mildred's successive visits helped considerably.)

My mother-in-law, meanwhile, looked down from heaven and found it good—well, most of it. Don't fret, Lucy, I put the basters down at the foot where I can tuck it under the mattress.

Spring

I hold the sudden breaking up of winter
   in my cupped hands
spring stirs in urgent circles
breathing and beating in bareness
raising all the nerve ends in a growing
going circle after circle
a wave length into night
buds reaching
and teaching all the new birds
   still sleeping
how to sing

—Mary Jean Irion,
"March Night"

Blue Denim Diary

I am not given to collecting "coffee-table books," but one offering of recent years I find irresistible—*The Country Diary of an Edwardian Lady*, a reproduction of a diary actually kept and illustrated in 1906 by a talented English gentlewoman, Edith Holden. The drawings are lovely, the text informative, the whole interspersed with appropriate bits of poetry and prose. I dreamed over it in the bookshops a year or two, then gave it to myself as a gift for the soul's lifting.

My spirits are amply nourished in the fields, meadows, and woods of my own "estate," but I often find myself consulting the *Country Diary* as a botanical reference and reflecting upon how different *this* country woman's diary would read. . . .

113

April 20: To church in a.m. Worked in p.m. digging (with potato digger) black plastic in which last year's melons were planted, Paul retrieving plastic, Pat operating digger. Serious strain on thirty-year marriage. Peace restored on excursion to woods to dig beech trees. Trees transplanted to yard, Paul digging, Pat advising. Puppy chasing canoes on river. To Mill Hollow in evening to search for pup.

April 21: Cooler. Paul plowing. Peace prolonged with picnic by pond at high noon—egg salad sandwiches and Chablis. Sunny and warm out of wind. Frog music and the voice of the turtle heard in our land. To valley in p.m. with friend Emily in search of other spring wonders: bloodroot, adder's tongue, skunk cabbage. Doe appears from river, white tail waving like flag of truce. Paul planting peas (sixty pounds) as we return to house. Lungwort and primrose blooming under lilacs as I fertilize borders. Friend Bessie to supper and to work with us on quilt afterward. Paul quilts two blocks to my one. Tsch!

April 22: Paul up at 3:00 taking potatoes to market. Pat out in morning spreading ammonium nitrate on rye. Thatcher chasing after tractor all day—blond pup, green rye, blue sky, jet passing over. Looking up, glad I'm not on it.

> *You know how it is with an April day*
> *When the sun is out and the wind is still,*
> *You're one month on in the middle of May.*

> —Robert Frost,
> "Two Tramps in Mudtime"

Afternoon, Pat dragging ground with springtooth and cultipacker (thirtieth year). "Don't turn too short," says Paul, following after, planting an acre of beans, four acres sweet corn. To Oberlin in evening, gussied up and flushed with sunburn, for Cleveland Orchestra. Worn from the weight of two tons of nitrate, fall asleep through dissonance of Sir Wm. Walton. Awaken for Dvořák.

April 23: Over to Schuster place with ammonium and spreader again. Collect trash along roadside. Bake sour cream cookies at noon. Down to creek in late afternoon to pick cowslips (marsh marigolds) for friend Vivian on birthday. Think of Mama, who loved them so. Daffodils blooming wildly along road by potato barn.

A poet could not but be gay
In such a jocund company . . .
And then my heart with pleasure fills,
And dances with the daffodils.

—William Wordsworth,
"I Wandered Lonely as a Cloud"

What a gift Don Kropp gave us when he planted them there twenty-five years ago. Don moved on to greener pastures, but the daffodils flourish where he left them. Meeting on estate planning in the evening. Rushed home to watch *Henry V* on PBS. Great!

April 24: Paul to Cleveland market in night. Cold at 6:00 a.m. when I go out in ski clothes to seed clover. Brrr!

A cloud comes over the sunlit arch
And you're two months back in the middle of March.

Wheat seeded by airplane in the soybeans last fall emerges now in rows. Clover will settle into frost cracks and emerge among the ripening wheat. Out in the evening to speak for Fair Board at Holiday Inn. Ran out of gas on freeway. Phoned Paul at midnight. "Honey . . . !" Came with pickup and fuel. Less than cordial.

April 25: Paul up at 3:00 and to market again. Still sounds less than cordial this morning. "Too cold to work outside. Let's get this bedroom papered." Measure and cut together, Pat pastes, Paul hangs paper. (Easier than digging plastic.) Room ready now for quilt. Midnight gas run forgiven. Harmony prevails. Afternoon, Paul fits potato ground. Pat mends coveralls, writes. College boys return in early evening to find parents quilting in the quiet under the lamplight. To bed early (odeur de new wallpaper), potato planting tomorrow. . . .

Fiscal Insecurity

Way back in time, before guidance counselors, high school students got some pretty shoddy advice. I was advised, for example, that a girl going on to college need not trouble her pretty head about bookkeeping. The assumption was that Mr. Right would come along and carry her off to a preppy island of fiscal security where she could raise a manicured hand demurely to her cheek and sigh, "I just can't make head or tail of this checkbook."

Forty years later I'm still struggling to understand "straight line depreciation" and "capital debt repayment capacity." I am perpetually baffled by reports of corporate earnings. How does Ford Motor Company continue to exist and prosper, for example, when it loses five or ten million a quarter?

One winter I went with Paul to a skull session on the computerized records the Production Credit Association keeps of our farm operation. They're terribly impressive, those records. I held them up and measured them the way you measure yard goods, from the tip of the nose to the end of the arm. Three and a half yards!

The income portion is relatively brief. Three and a half inches— $114,000. Zowie! That is followed by about two and a half feet of expenses, which total $89,000. Hmm. . . . That leaves $25,000 as net income. But we're not through yet. Things get very murky as we move into "capital assets."

Holy smoke! Look at that list of assets! Seventy-eight items— tractors, bulk wagons, potato cutters, tile, irrigation pipe, ponds, sheds—everything there, I think, but the outhouse, each listed with a figure for depreciation. We seem to have $19,000 worth of depreciation, which I suppose must be subtracted from net income. Now we're down to $6,000. That should qualify us for food stamps!

On one of the last pages of analysis I find some interesting statistics, labeled, "Return to labor, management, and assets." There's one especially intriguing item: "Return to unpaid family labor: a minus $64,990!" If there is one thing I understand about these balance sheets it's the identity of the "unpaid family labor," and I will testify for a fact that I received a minus $64,990 last year.

I'm beginning to understand the Ford Motor Company's loss of earnings statements. I'm also formulating a concessions and wage package for next year for the "unpaid family labor." I'm going to demand the right to be listed on the depreciation schedule. I see notes after some of those items that say "junked." Others are marked "sold," still others, "replaced."

I am none of the above, and I'm at least as much of an asset as a bin stacker. I say I belong on there. I figure I've got at least twenty good years yet. And I'm going to demand that my salary be raised to a minus $300,000!

Green Pleas

My flowering maple has just "molted" for the third time this year.

There is white mite in the schefflera. The underleaves of the African violet rot and sag limply on the rims of their pots. The aloe plant falls rootless from its potting soil.

Each time a shoot sprouts hopefully from the apex of the rubber plant, a great leaf peels from the lower end, leaving a longer, spindlier stock. The lemon geranium sloughs dry brown leaves at the base of its branches. The dwarf palms, too, extract a brown frond in ransom for each new and tender shoot. The philodendron shows yellow evidence of overwatering, and the jade plant pants for lack of moisture, dropping fleshy green blobs around the base of the plant stand.

For twenty-five years of life as a housewife I survived nicely with not so much as an ivy to complicate my life. Once or twice a green plant intruded for a spell, surrendering its life in payment for the privilege.

Then in the winter of '76 I innocently accepted a small jade plant from a friend. All amateurs know that a jade is invincible. Yet by summer it had dropped its fat leaves and I thought I had done it in sufficiently. I set it out for discard, and lo! It flourished.

Discarding a live plant is like drowning a kitten, so I nursed the jade in my hit-and-miss way. Sometimes when I spoke for a banquet, they'd give me the centerpiece, often a green plant. Once I nursed a gigantic philodendron from San Diego to Aspen, to Minneapolis, and thence to a neglected spot in the living room, where it languishes.

So they came—these plants. Relatives die and people console you with plants, so you tend them, haphazardly. Kids come home from college, no longer sure what the motivation was that gave rise to Christmas cactus, wandering Jew, or maidenhair fern. Mom adopts them. Plants emerge as favors at bridal showers and prizes at Tupperware parties.

What have I done to deserve all this chlorophyll? I never asked to be William Beebe, never intentionally invited even one of these green monsters here to share my limited space and squander my time. Why is it that now I am enslaved by them?

Is there nowhere a comforting support group, an Overplant Tenders Anonymous for harried souls like me? More important—is there no battered plant shelter, no Endangered Species Society where these helpless green things may seek haven from neglect, where they can find the regular care, the tender musings, the overdue fertilizer, and the Plant Shine that are their due?

Somewhere out there is a foundation in search of a charity, a philanthropist in search of a cause. I am sounding a plea. Take up that great big watering can before it's too late. When all these innocents are dead, their spent protoplasm will stain your hands.

Oldie but Goodie

Some desperate soul once called me, asking, "What do they do with their old typewriters over at the *Chronicle?*"

"They type on them," I said without hesitation.

"Well, how about you?" he said.

"Me too. I type on my old typewriter," I said.

That was ten years ago, and though most of the battered wrecks at the paper have given way to computer consoles, Pat Leimbach is still banging away at her old Royal Standard. That is, she was . . . until 2:14 this morning when something went "zap!" The carriage sprang sharply to the left, the ribbon cases whirred audibly, and the rest was silence. You could press the keys, but no glorious type marched in triumph across the page.

I laughed nervously, as you laugh when you are startled by something foolish in the night. And then I laughed robustly, thinking of the delight Paul and Orrin would take in this event. For eight years they've been nagging . . . "Ma, you promised that if we made any money on our first book, we'd buy a decent typewriter." And already there'd been a second book, and the old Royal had limped valiantly on.

I thought briefly of laying a sprig of laurel on the carriage and breathing a benediction, but surrender does not come easily to aficionados of old typewriters. What is it about a manual typewriter that holds us? Does the greater physical quality of manual type better suit the mental intensity of writing? Or is it simply association buildup, the comfort of the familiar?

An editor friend was once showing me about her elegant Philadelphia apartment, resplendent with paintings, antiques, Oriental rugs. There in her study, alone on a polished desk like an art object, sat a sixty-year-old typewriter in mint condition, the one she still used.

She tendered it the sort of reverence she held for the mentors who had led her to great success in her field, and none would have questioned her loyalty.

Mine is no art object. It's dusty and neglected and sits in a quagmire of clerical disorder. I'm not even very skilled at operating it, preferring to think with a broad-lined ballpoint. But when I want to type, I want something that responds! But now . . . what?

Perhaps all was not lost. Maybe resuscitation was still a possibility. When morning came, I hauled it to Mr. Baker, who runs a reliable old typewriter establishment on 2nd Street in Elyria. I hoped the fellows wouldn't notice it was missing and put a hex on it.

"That's an old one you've got there," said Mr. Baker. "Let's see . . . it was made in the early thirties, so that's fifty years it's seen. You don't have a piece of machinery on your farm that's given you comparable service. With a little maintenance it'll last you another fifty years."

Poor Orrin, craving an IBM Selectric, now to be told that this typewriter is going to live longer than his mother.

"Well, it's pretty dead at the moment," I said, indicating a long, mysterious piece of woven tape that dangled from its side.

"Not serious. Not serious at all. I'll have that fixed for you in a matter of minutes."

"It came originally from the school over to Brownhelm," I said. "My mother-in-law was on the school board, and . . ."

"Oh yes!" said Mr. Baker, his face brightening. "I sold them those machines back in the happy times. Yessir, this is one of my machines. They couldn't afford new ones, but I sold them six of these reconditioned ones at $60 apiece. And, you know, if you sold that machine today, reconditioned as it was then, it would still be worth $60."

Not if you sold it to Orrin, I was thinking.

"There wasn't any typing room in those days, so they used the science lab. Had to get the typewriters all covered up and put away in time for biology. Remember Mead Petty? Over at Henrietta?" Ah . . . Henrietta, the little school down Route 511 from Brownhelm, the school where I first taught and where I met Paul. I remembered everything about Henrietta.

"Indeed I do," I said. "Mead Petty ran the tile yard there. Splendid fellow. He was still a community patriarch when I went to teach at Henrietta."

"Well, Mead was president of the school board, and I remember the night they were deliberating over whether to purchase typewrit-

119

ers. We sat there till midnight, and the board was deadlocked, two and two. Mead said finally, 'Well, I'll put my neck on the line. Those children need typewriters.' So he voted to break the tie, and they bought their first typewriters—four of them. Reconditioned like Brownhelm's, $60 each. Yes, those were the happy times. People pulling together. . . . Now let's see what we can do for this typewriter. Looks as if it could do with a bit of cleaning. . . ."

There are a lot of good reasons for hanging on to an old typewriter —none better than Mr. Baker. Orrin went the following week to retrieve my typewriter, and even he has to agree.

Season of the Lemmings

The state university has screeched to a halt for spring break, and all those homesick youngsters have piled into the family car with their dirty laundry, their guitars, and their pop rock tapes to go home and gladden the hearts of adoring parents and hometown beaux. Right? Ho, ho, ho!

Yesterday I dropped Orrin off in a Columbus alley with a duffle bag and a CB and a rented wet suit, beside a decrepit van loaded to its bubble top with sleeping bags and oxygen tanks and pimply kids looking unsure of where they were going and what they were going to do when they got there.

A scuba trip to Florida had sounded like a timely idea when Orrin introduced it a couple of weeks back. The objective, as nearly as I could determine, was to get certified as divers. Then he showed me the weighted belt and the twelve-inch knife ("in case you get caught in a net or chased by a barracuda") and started talking about bubbles in the blood and nitrogen narcosis and getting the bends, and it came through to me that scuba diving was different from snorkeling.

"Who's running this show?" I asked, with the sort of nonchalance you must feign when you know you're nineteen years late with your mothering. Now I stood face to face with the answer. The scuba instructor, perfunctorily introduced as "Rich," was not a figure to instill confidence. He had thin, stringy, chlorine-bleached hair, steel-rimmed glasses over beady eyes, and a midsection that spilled over his belt fore and aft. The one piece of assurance I had been given by Orrin was that "he doesn't drink."

"Do you know where you're going?" I had asked. (A philosophical question, I see in retrospect.)

"Naw, he's got some names of beaches, but no towns. There's one nude beach we heard about, but we don't know if we'll go there or not." This was not exactly going to be a Maupintour, I judged.

"And just twelve guys?" I asked with incredulity.

"Yeah, but I think I've got that problem all worked out. The girl who cuts my hair is leaving for Florida the same afternoon with twelve girls," said Orrin with a smile.

If I hadn't had the utmost faith in Orrin's capacity to organize and take charge of the whole bunch of them, as tour guide and all, I would have taken him by the ear and towed him home with me. I left him a stamped, self-addressed envelope for a progress report, but I figure I'll be lucky to get as much as a "Glub, glub, glub. . . ."

As for our other collegian, Ted pulled out early this morning, heading for Tennessee in somebody's camper with his new Kawasaki 250, his leather breeches, his Bell helmet, his Scott goggles, his Hi-Point boots, and forty or fifty pounds of other racing gear to sweep the first of the year's motorcycle trials.

"Have I ever got a hot cycle this year, Mom. I'm gonna blow 'em all in the weeds," said my six-foot Adonis.

All I could think of as I watched him disappear in the morning mist was the wispy little fellow of long ago with the pointed face and the braces on his turned-in feet and the worries I had about what would become of him.

What I should have been worrying about was spring break fifteen years later and the fate of two parents looking out to the children's playground where the base lines on the ball diamond have all grown to grass.

Scarf Tossing

The Easter parade has once more passed by, and I did not make the rotogravure. I sat in my accustomed pew (second from the front on the left), feeling rather foxy in an end-of-winter sale dress that had been marked down three times.

Before the "Gloria" had died away, one of my more stylish friends bent over me, saying, "Let's just tuck this price tag down inside your collar, shall we?" It gives one a certain sympathy for the guy who forgets to zip his fly.

I should be resigned to my image as country klutz, but the ego is a relentless tyrant. What frumpy little person is there who does not yearn for flair, the ability to toss a scarf about the shoulders with insouciance and look like Cheryl Tieg? I wrap a scarf around my neck and look like Miss Piggy with the croup.

Betty Ford once made a brief appearance on television demonstrating a half dozen ways to tie a scarf, which explains why she got to be the President's wife and I did not. Any woman who can tie a scarf in a half dozen ways deserves to be First Lady.

I have an awesome collection of scarves, most of which I've never worn beyond the confines of my bedroom.

I fold and drape them, toss them over my shoulders, secure them with stunning old dull-pinned brooches inherited from great-aunts. I appraise myself, recognizing that I look quite a bit like Whistler's Mother, and unpin, remove, and fold them away.

My friend Alida has a master's degree in scarf tying. "How do you keep those darned things in place?" I have ventured a few times.

"With pins," she says, quite simply.

I've tried it, and it isn't simple. I've had some success pinning them to my bra straps, but that's a good way to develop a tick. Pin them to the collar and someone's bound to ask sooner or later, "Did you mean to have that pin showing?"

I fully expect that when the undertaker lays me out, someone will gaze reverently down and say, "Doesn't she look nice? But maybe we could tie that scarf with a little more pizzazz."

Sic Transit Gloria

A few minutes' trolley ride from the center of most of our large cities is a once-stylish area of large homes, fastidiously constructed and landscaped for America's empire builders in a lavish era of conspicuous consumption by the few. They were in their time monuments to luxury: carved woodwork, paneled studies, leaded glass windows, crystal chandeliers, spacious foyers, ornate ballustrades, marble fireplaces, parquet floors, ceramic baths with brass fittings, butler's pantries, and servants' quarters with separate stairways.

There is a curious irony in the fact that most of these extravagant dwellings have in recent times been taken over by the have-nots. The new tenants are a polyglot bunch—black, white, Hispanic—not all down-and-out, not all stable families after the former mold, either. Often they are students or young people fresh from college pooling their parents' early attic pieces and putting together an apartment in a walled-off wing, a divided upstairs, or a third-floor loft. Sometimes they are young couples with a baby, who is hauled up and down an outside stair on daily trips to and from the babysitter's so that his parents can ply their professions. Sometimes they are alternate-lifestyle folks existing in odd combinations. All take a fierce pride in the mix of the area, finding as much satisfaction in their detachment as the original occupants did in their interdependence.

Whoever they are, lacking gardeners and butlers, upstairs and downstairs maids, and a pipeline to the bank, the new inhabitants of these turn-of-the-century showplaces live life differently than it was planned to be lived here. And the lovely old properties have taken on a functional, down-at-the-heels appearance. I have on a number of occasions been a guest in these "holding areas" of faded elegance, visiting young relatives or the children of friends, and had opportunities to study the evolution that proceeds here.

The grand old appointments are usually irrelevant in the eyes of the present dwellers. The high ceilings are seen as energy-extravagant. The fireplaces seldom work and are a long distance from the expensive wood supply. The chimney sweeps no longer come around in their top hats and tails. All the tenants have been at least mildly influenced by the natural-food movement and seem to feel they can make some economies in the food bill. The rose garden has given way to zucchini and cherry tomatoes.

High priority is put on pets—usually a dog, the larger and fiercer the safer. He may well have played havoc with the remaining landscaping, and a chain-link fence is threaded through the boxwoods. Gone are the limousines and touring cars tucked away in shiny splendor in ginger-bread carriage houses. Today the driveways are crowded with custom pickups, jeeps, vans, and small foreign cars—one vehicle per occupant, to be parked who knows where on snow days.

Within, the places are potted jungles of green plants, the hallmark of the new breed. Furnishings show evidence of Saturdays spent at auctions and garage sales. There is usually an ambiguous plan to refinish them on some hazy morrow. Curtains and drapes are, by and large, immaterial. Bamboo blinds or shutters are in high favor. Low

priority is put on clean windows, but sterile bathrooms show telltale
evidence that these young people were reared in white tennis shoes
with clean underwear daily and that flossing after meals is a life-and-
death matter.

The stereo system occupies the sort of prominence once accorded
the Oriental rugs and the objets d'art shipped home in mahogany
packing cases from the Far East.

The kitchens, blandly designed for hired help, usually come in for
some upgrading by the new tenants. There has been a limited attempt made to transform them into the sort of cozy functional place
that Mom enjoys back home, though that is almost the only conces-
sion to Mom and "back home." (With the exception of that sterile
bathroom.)

The largest overall difference between these homes today and yesterday is that nothing is designed or chosen or placed to be permanent. These dear old places are destined to be waiting stations on the
way to somewhere else.

Any day of the week this or that tenant may say to a friend,
"Whatta ya say we synchronize our speakers, cross-pollinate our pa-
pyrus, merge our macramé?" And the moving begins. . . .

Parlor Maid

Out in Kansas the wheat is heading two weeks early and the farm
ponds are dry. At Bible study sessions the prayers are for rain, and
everybody from the village doctor to the clerk at the Dairy Queen
expresses "rainful" hopes.

So it was a good day when I awakened last week on the Headley
dairy farm near Ellsworth, Kansas, to find rain doing a staccato beat
on the tin roof.

"Did you really want to get up and help milk?" asked my hostess,
sticking her blond head in the door of the frilly bedroom from which
I had displaced the family daughter.

"Yup, I do," said I, swinging my feet from under the pink sheets
onto the pink carpet, stretching, and wondering if I was really in my
right mind. I pulled on blue jeans and a flannel shirt, long socks and
rubber boots (borrowed from my hostess). Then out into the rainy
predawn we went and down the muddy little slope to the barn.

Rance Headley was already ushering his "ladies" into the milking parlor as I entered by a narrow door off the bulk tank room. I flattened myself against the wall as the steaming beasts lumbered up over the sill, swung their huge heads to the left and to the right, sized up the situation, then filed routinely into one of the eight stanchions flanking the central milking pit. Good obedient creatures they seemed, only now and then requiring a smack on the rump or a poke in the ribs to move into milking position.

Jeanine took up a hose and quickly sprayed the udders hanging at eye level in front of us. Then she went back over each, concentrating carefully on the teats, wiping them finally with a paper towel. Rance attached the milkers with their four nozzles that actually squeeze the milk down from the udder. By watching the glass collection cup on the base of the milker and feeling the udder, the experienced person knows when to remove the milker. "Untouched by human hand," the milk surges through the Pyrex pipeline into a large holding bottle at the end of the milking parlor, thence to the refrigerated bulk tank in the next room.

Watching this young couple go efficiently about the process of milking their large herd, I thought of my mother long ago sitting by lantern light on her milk stool in the old cow shed below the hill, her head pressed against the right rear flank of our Jersey cow, wearily doing the evening milking. Much as I teased, she wouldn't teach me to milk, fearing, she said, that I might have to do it for life. Strange that I should be here on this May morning almost envying these two the unity that comes with surrender to a productive, disciplined, and consuming task.

Perhaps the only annoyance common to that long-ago cow shed and this sophisticated milking parlor is the pesky flicking of the cow's tails.

"Look out," hollered Jeanine as she shielded me from a gooshy fly whisk.

I shuffled about, trying to avoid the busy twosome as they moved the milkers from one bank of cows to the other. When each group of four was finished, a gate was opened and they ambled out. Rance then went with his long switch and chased in four more.

Jeanine ran back to the house a couple of times to wake the children and get them off to school, so I took over the simplest of the jobs, the toweling of the teats. At first I shrank from the intimacy of the task, but the gentle creatures stood patiently, grateful for the imminent relief to their swollen udders. As I grew more comfortable with the work I was overcome by a strange tenderness for these clumsy and generous beasts.

As each milker was removed, I lifted a cup of disinfectant to the teats, a safeguard against bacteria between milkings.

"Hey, this one's only got three hickeys," I said. "How come?"

"Another cow stepped on it when she was lying down," said Rance. "Tore it right off. But even with three teats she's an outstanding producer, so we keep her."

"Oooo." I winced.

Rance and Jeanine commented on the various cows as they attached and detached the milkers.

"Gee, can you recognize them just by their udders?"

"We sure can. And each cow has her name and her peculiarities."

"Wow! This one has a firm udder," I said as I finished cleaning number four on the left.

"That's Daisy II. She averages 105 pounds of milk a day."

I figured in my head a moment. . . . "Holy cow! That's over thirteen gallons. What a wonderful milk machine."

Three hours passed as we worked quietly in the warm, damp enclosure. The mingling smells of manure and milk and silage grew less and less offensive till I ceased to notice them altogether. Rance moved in and out in his rubber boots, commenting happily on the torrents of rain.

At last he announced the seventy-second and final cow. Jeanine hosed down the milking parlor, Rance set the milkers onto the cleansing apparatus and turned on the mechanism that flushes and sterilizes the whole shebang, and we went in to breakfast.

Later in the morning I borrowed some stationery from Jeanine. There on the letterhead was Daisy II, Holstein extraordinaire. Under her picture, Psalm 118, verse 23: "This is the Lord's doing; it is marvelous in our eyes." Indeed.

Semantics Antics

Things are not going well on the committee to revise the church constitution. A schism seems to be forming around "deacons" and "deaconesses." If there is a board of elders composed of six men and six women (supposedly performing the same duties), should they be called deacons and deaconesses, or should they all be deacons?

The minister proposes that they be deacons and that the constitution specify "six men and six women." The male chauvinists on the committee say, "Fine. Call them deacons if you will, but doggone it, don't specify whether they're men or women. If you want men and women, then leave them as deacons and deaconesses."

Relevant to the issue, of course, is the fact that the minister is female. She is not, as she points out, a "ministress," though she is clearly subject to stress, and if the controversy persists, it's not going to be mini-stress. Germane also is the fact that we've gone a few rounds in these liberating years over "chairperson," and "Our Father, God," and other terms seen as having sexual bias. Clearly there will be no end of controversy until the congregation ratifies an inclusive language Bible or until hell freezes over, whichever occurs first. Till then we must muddle through.

Ex-Deaconess Leimbach, female chauvinist, is riding the fence, trying to decide whether conceding to "deacon" means she's gaining or losing ground where equality is concerned. If I reject "chairman" because it falls into the male bailiwick, then why do I want to be a "deacon," which has a clearly male connotation?

Yet there's a lot of excess verbiage in forever referring to "the Board of Deacons and Deaconesses." The writer in me says let's simplify.

My husband is threatening to leave me, or the church, or both of us, if I capitulate to "deacons." My other male chauvinist friends, likewise. Should the church split over the issue (Our Mother, God, forbid!), we could become embroiled in paradox.

We could conceivably become the Reformed Church of the Deaconess and the Church of the Latterday Deacons. The male chauvinists would then align themselves with the Deaconess Church, and the female chauvinists with the Deacons.

The question we should probably be addressing is this: Should the "deaconesses" all become "deacons," who would wash the communion cups?

Dingdong Bell Tone

What really bothered me about getting a hearing aid was not that it would destroy my good looks, but that folks would think I was feeble-minded. My early impressions of people with those strange contraptions in their ears and wires running down inside their collars, out their shirtfronts to their pockets, was that they weren't quite "with it." I suppose it was an impression based on the fact that early hearing aids weren't terribly effective and communication with those who wore them was still limited. By the time I was old enough to make a mature appraisal, it was too late. That early prejudice had put down roots.

I've had hearing problems since my mid-thirties and have certainly learned how easily one is intimidated when the conversation is passing unheard. You really have to struggle to retain your concept of self! You might easily give the impression of being dim-witted.

So now I am come to hearing aids, and I want the record to state that this funny-looking thing in my ear has opened a whole new world. And I'm not speaking merely of a new awareness of the *old* world.

It's no great joy to recognize that my refrigerator is running most of the time, or that the humidifier makes one heck of a racket, or that there's a constant hum in the bathroom radiator. I was not especially rewarded to learn that some kind of motor sings lullabies to the mice in the furnace room. And nobody enjoys hair that crinkles or clothes that crackle. No, it's not the augmentation of the old sounds that intrigues me, but my new James Bondish involvement in everybody else's conversations.

For example, en route home with my new "ear" I stopped for lunch near the university. Across the restaurant I heard a lady talking to the maitre d' about all the weight she'd lost on the diet of the moment. He proceeded to recommend the high-carbohydrate pasta.

At the table facing me a college instructor was sealing the fate of some hapless coed. "She has a lot of ability, but she's trying to get by on her looks."

Behind me in the bar some guy was into the political scene. "Write his memoirs! Why, you'd think he'd want to forget!"

The fellows at the table next to the prof were ordering scotch Manhattans and asking about the veal. At the table beyond them a big investor was making sad concessions over his martini. "Yeah, I sold that stock two days too soon. But I can't complain. I made a few nickels. When I called my broker this morning, he said . . ." When E. F. Hutton talks, you don't even have to leave your seat. Just crank up your hearing aid a peg or two.

The best feature of the hearing aid, I discovered as it became user-friendly, is that you can turn it off. And if you wear two of them, as I now do, you can retreat at will to a "quiet room" no matter where you are. (The hearing aid in place serves as an earplug to screen out what little natural hearing you might have.)

I find this a great weapon against the rock music that increasingly assaults me in shopping malls and grocery stores. There *are* times when seeming to be feeble-minded is a total irrelevancy. My hearing aids also eliminate a lot of arguments at home when I need a quiet work area and the house doesn't seem big enough. Phone conversations are less disturbed by family noises if one shuts off the opposite aid.

A hearing aid is also a good conversation starter. Many people are sensitive about wearing hearing aids and are relieved to find somebody so happy with her own that she will discuss them at will. If Ronald Reagan and I ever get off in a corner together, you can bet we'll be discussing the relative merits of "in the ear" and "over the ear."

"This hearing aid could change your life," said the affable guy who sold me my first one. "One of my customers came in and said she was filing for divorce. She discovered that the 'business associate' he'd been talking to on the phone all these months was really his lover. By adjusting the power on her hearing aid she could hear both sides of the conversation."

And all this time I thought Paul was talking to the Crop Reporting Service!

Geography Lesson—Updated

Back in fourth grade when Miss Drechsler led us into the wonder world of geography, she used to encourage the making of those relief maps modeled of sticky, salt-flour clay, painted erratically and studded with cotton bales, logs, potatoes, sheep, pigs, or whatever symbol suited the region. One remarkable spring week (forty-five years later) I wandered the West and Midwest checking out Miss Drechsler's facts.

I rolled big, round hay bales across North Dakota amid flocks of sheep and herds of cattle. I set corn shocks on Iowa and chased hogs among them. I scattered cattle along the mountain slopes of Wyoming and dropped sheaves of wheat on the high plateaus of eastern

Idaho. Where once we smeared yellow desert in central Idaho, I put a new symbol, an irrigation sprinkler, and strewed potatoes. I daubed white snow on the loftiest peaks of the Rockies and on the mountain sides drew little pine triangles. Yes, it's all there much as Miss D. envisioned it for us.

But the facts of the matter seldom convey the poetry. It's a glorious country and never lovelier than in early June. I flew to Bismarck in North Dakota and drove southwest to a town called New England through the Elysian fields themselves, the most luxuriant green grass I ever hope to see. The rolling hills and the distant buttes shimmered in variegated greens. I came up over a rise and looked out across a terraced valley. Unbelievable! The most beautiful place in the world. Why were my eyes watering?

The next day, Iowa. Driving eastward from Omaha I got lost, as I enjoy doing when the sun is shining and the time is loose, along the Nishnabotna (Indian for "deep enough to float a canoe").

Iowa was in several of its endless corn phases. Some was in sacks on the back of pickup trucks, some was being planted, some beneath the combed ground germinating, some just a whisper of green around a terraced hillside, and some already swayed in the wind—a tapestry of delicate geometrics. Nope, I was wrong. This is it—the most beautiful spot in the world.

Two days later I drove across Idaho, eastward from Boise along the base of the Sawtooth range. Here the greens were tinted with blue and purple, mile after mile of sage with lavender-blue lupine between, here and there a hillside yellow with mustard. The clouds were from the pages of once-upon-a-time, and the shadowed hills were unreal, mysterious. Here, after all, is the most beautiful place. . . .

The following day I was in Wyoming. I came down along the high plain beside the Snake River, looking across yellow-green meadows through a fringe of swaying aspens to the glory of the Grand Teton range. Oh . . . this is what beauty is all about!

I wound up then over the Tetons, down across the Snake once more, and along a valley into which rushed cold mountain streams on smooth pebble beds. Then I climbed again, up, up, up, westward toward Idaho Falls. At the summit the setting sun shone on a heaven of rolling wheat fields, mile after mile after mile, stretching north and south of the highway into the very sky. Shangri La.

Back in Ohio the peas were swelling in the pods and the potato vines were row to row. The roadsides and lanes were glorified with dandelions. Light filtered into my kitchen through the soft, green shade of the honey locust, the linden was in bloom and its sweet smell permeated the house. What place is lovelier than this?

It's a wonderland, Miss Drechsler. Print A M E R I C A across it.

A Case of Character

I've been out casing the luggage departments of late, searching for graduation gifts—zipping zippers, buckling buckles, latching latches, and scratching my head. Every graduate with promise of going somewhere is entitled to a good suitcase, and I enjoy giving them, for that involves me vicariously in the going. But finding a suitcase that measures up to my standards is a tough order.

I sometimes think they only made one—mine. Or is it mine? After thirty-one years of continuous family use, my boxy blue suitcase has probably moved into something akin to public domain. A good suitcase packs a lot of memories and a quantity of dreams. My brothers and sisters crowded the living room the night of my college graduation, watching with pride as I unwrapped that splendid blue suitcase with the wooden frame and the white leather trim. Splitting the price six ways had still cost them a bundle, so I valued their gift despite nagging fears that I might never again leave the county.

The beauty of this particular suitcase is that is has room inside. Today's cases have pockets and pouches and zippered inserts, straps and wheels and hangers and whole compartments that detach, but there's precious little uncommitted space to put the kind of things I've discovered good suitcases must house:

A bride's trousseau, a beach blanket, a bottle of port.
All of a baby's layette between babies.
A grandchild's travel pack: little boy's overalls, sleepers, training pants, rubber boots, teddy bear, security blanket, baby bottles, and dress-up clothes for church.
A Delft teapot, two cups and saucers, a crystal vase, clothes for a six-weeks' idyll, and a bottle of Austrian schnapps.
Three weeks of a college boy's rank laundry.
Motorcycle boots and leathers, a set of metric wrenches, goggles, gloves, a plastic fender, a headlight, a greasy chain in a plastic bag, and a bottle of goggle defogger.

Ski boots, parkas, stretch pants, woolen underwear, mittens, caps, sweaters, a ski map of Snowmass, a hot water bottle, and a jug of Hearty Burgundy.

There is no contemporary suitcase that you can stretch between two stateroom bunks to play a hand of bridge or spread with a towel for a picnic table on the Côte d' Azur or use as a writing desk in a cramped pension.

I just tripped over the old blue suitcase in the back room, where it was dropped late last night by a returning student. Its scarred surfaces are adorned with stickers: "THE POTATO, THE INCREDIBLE EDIBLE, LORAIN COUNTY FAIR, OHIO STATE UNIVERSITY, CERIANI SHOCKS, HI-POINT ACCESSORIES, KAWASAKI MOTORCYCLES, BING CARBURETORS, INTERNATIONAL SIX DAYS TRIALS, BEAT MICHIGAN.

Inside, the trappings of a new era: a wet suit, a weight belt, a pressure gauge, and scuba flippers.

The remnants of an old Cunard Line tourist seal still whisper of a memorable crossing on the *Queen Mary*, but the rest of the story can be constructed from nicks and scratches, smudges and stains, and the broad band of silver duct tape bandaging one corner. The white leather is yellowed, and half the satin lining is gone (sacrificed to a leaking bottle of cod liver oil). But the frame is still square, the hinges and latches function, and the leather handle is intact.

No, you can't buy that kind of suitcase today. Occasionally as I watch the river of luggage that pours onto airport carousels, I spot a piece that bears signs of having been loved and lived with like our "old blue." My heart warms in contemplation of the people and the places it has known. A suitcase takes on character with the breadth and depth of its living and ahh, the tales it could tell. . . .

Summer

I am not bound for any public place,
but for ground of my own
where I have planted vines
and orchard trees,
And in the heat of the day climbed up
into the healing shadow
of the woods.
Better than any argument
is to rise at dawn and pick
dew-wet red berries in a cup.

—"A Standing Ground,"
Wendell Berry

High on the Vine

"The difference between the rich and the poor is vegetables," said some astute observer of the scene—Truman Capote, I think—the implication being that people with cultivated tastes know and appreciate good vegetables and are willing and able to afford them.

My mother wasn't rich, but she had a great respect for vegetables and prepared them superbly. We ate like the Duke and Duchess of Windsor. I think of her each June as I hustle my fresh young peas into the freezer.

I remember being sent to deliver a kettle of creamed new peas as a gesture of condolence to a home where they'd had a death. At the time it impressed me as a strange offering, but in retrospect I know those peas were more welcome than a dozen angel food cakes.

I calculate my young peas at a dollar a pint (excluding labor) and well worth the cost. We raise them for market, so I feel I can afford the luxury. When I say young, I mean downright premature. By the time they fill the pods, they're beginning to lose their delicate sweetness. When the morning's load comes from the field, I search it for the baskets with thinner pods, the ones picked by the beginners. Paul grumbles about the "darned kids" who pick them so young, but I rejoice.

It isn't just the flavor of this supreme vegetable or the anticipation of winter feasts that gives me pleasure, but the whole June ambience. It's a season of high hopes. The crops are coming along in great style, still outdistancing the weeds. The first potato blossoms are opening. The spring rains have established grass in places where grass will wither in late summer. The wheat is heading and hinting of yellow, and the fragrance of linden and honeysuckle scent the air.

Spirits are high and kids are eager. It's not difficult to coax Leslie and Kelly from their porch across the road to come sit under the maples and shell peas. Their fresh young faces and secretive giggles are part and parcel of the pleasure. Paul and Orrin come from their field work and flop down to help. The dogs lie companionably at our sides. I wonder what the poor people are doing today.

Comin' Up Roses

On Sunday afternoon, July 1, at the Clear Creek Church of Christ, Merle and Beulah Eichelberger celebrated their fortieth wedding anniversary in the company of family, friends, neighbors, and church folk. Out front, beneath the pine trees dripping in a cold rain, Merle's '77 Chevy was bedecked in soggy bunting, the windows streaked with whitewash. Around the whitewalls of the tires in childish scrawl ran the gleeful pronouncement, "Just Married 40 Years." The authors of this mischief chased one another among the cars, oblivious of the drizzle, awaiting the predictable moment when Grandpa and Grandma would emerge and shriek in dismay.

The festivities were winding down as we descended the outside stairs, entered the "church parlors," and signed our names with red ink in the guest book. "Red is the color for the fortieth," said Beulah. Merle, who stepped forth to greet us then, had a red silk rose in his lapel, and Beulah wore a corsage of the same. The tables, gay with red and white streamers, had bud vases in the center holding silk rosebuds "all made by our daughter-in-law."

"Come over and have some punch," said Beulah. "We wanted something red for the punch table, and all I had was the material I bought for a dress when we was in Rome on our trip to the Holy Land." Under the Quaker lace cloth and the bowl of red punch and the red-rose-bedecked cake—the top layer had been carefully garnered on a small plate for some fresh-from-the-freezer future—was a length of brocade, red as a cardinal's robe, souvenir of a very high point in a frugal forty years.

"They took pictures of me and Merle cutting the cake. I told them it was the first time. Didn't have no cake the first wedding day. Went up to Monroe, Michigan, and got married. My sister-in-law, Lois, made the cake. She makes the most beautiful cakes. All kinds."

The ladies moved among the long tables, collecting Styrofoam punch cups and empty cake plates, or clustered in the kitchen "redding up": drying coffeepots, wiping counters, exchanging chatter about Merle and Beulah's day.

We sat then and had some red punch and a piece of Lois' rosebud cake. Merle brought the children to be introduced—Maxine, the home economics teacher; Larry, "who farms with us"; and Esther, the secretary. "Esther's wearing my wedding dress," said Beulah, indicating a dark-haired, soft-eyed girl in a white, short-sleeved, satin voile dress with longish, narrow skirt that called up late-Depression memories, ranging from rumble seats to the "Beer Barrel Polka."

"Come see the pictures," said Beulah, as the men talked together of herbicides and soybean prices. "Here we were ready to go up to Monroe." There was Merle at nineteen, looking too young to go into town for a block of ice, and Beulah in Esther's wedding dress, standing beside Merle's '37 Chevy coupe. "A whole bunch of us went up. Even Merle's grandmother. See? . . . This picture here.

"And here we was at Niagara Falls." Sure enough, there were the Canadian falls and two naive kids a long way from home. Then there were the children. One dress for three christenings at Clear Creek Church.

"These were the five houses we lived in," said Beulah, going on to give the locations. "Nearly starved in this place trying to go it alone. Then we started farming for a fellow. Saved enough to buy our first place. Then we bought that place and moved down there. Here's where we are now, and we're building a new house. Be ready when the snow flies, maybe. Farming over a thousand acres now.

Three hundred head of cattle. Got a good hired man. He went home to milk.

"Now this is Merle's parents' wedding picture . . . and these were my folks. Here's five generations of my family—my grandmother, my mother, me, Maxine, and her little girl. . . . Here's four generations from Merle's side. . . . Here's the children's wedding pictures. Maxine and her Larry. He's a preacher. They live over in Indiana. Came home for the day. Larry's going to preach for the evening service tonight.

"Here's the grandchildren. This one was just taken this morning before Sunday school.

"Here we were on our twentieth . . . and our thirtieth. The material in that blue dress came from the Philippines. Here's the picture that was in the paper."

By now the red silk roses had been collected into one big bunch. The punch table had been cleared. Out in the kitchen they were dividing leftover cake. Somebody—Lois?—was folding Beulah's Roman brocade.

"Hope nobody spilled anything on it," I said. "We'd better be moving on. You'll have to hustle if you're to get home for supper and back again for evening services."

"We're all going up to Savannah to the Harvest Table for supper. Real nice restaurant. Family style," said Beulah.

They stood in the doorway as we said goodbye. Behind them the set had been struck. The "church parlors" had reverted to cement block church basement. But all that red left a rosy glow.

Return to Eaglesmere

Driving eastward on I-80 three summers ago I took a detour north into a chapter from my past. In the summer of '46 I had worked as a waitress in a dignified inn on a mountain lake thirty-five miles from Muncy, Pennsylvania. After one's mind works for thirty years on an interlude from the flowering of youth it assumes such exaggerated proportions that it's rather a shock to seek out the setting and discover that it does indeed exist.

There in the center of Muncy was the Fort Brad Hotel (looking seedy but no seedier), where the bus put me down with suitcase and tennis racket. I passed a fitful night there, my first alone in any public lodging. Though I propped a chair against the door, I panicked at each footfall in the corridor, and morning was never so welcome. At 6:00 a.m. I rode out to the train station with the postman to meet two college friends, who were to have taken a Pullman up from Pittsburgh.

The train dropped off instead two traveling salesmen and a crate of chickens. The farmer's daughter and the traveling salesmen rode back to town sitting on the crate of chickens in the back of some farm woman's pickup truck. The two of them then hired a taxi and gave me a lift up to Eaglesmere, where they were headed for a jewelry convention. (My friends arrived later.)

The Crestmont Inn was the sort of traditional Eastern resort where the rich went to hobnob with the rich as their fathers and grandfathers had done before them, for a week, a month, or the whole summer.

Tennis played on well-groomed clay courts was the big pastime at the Crestmont. There were lessons with tennis pros, and late in summer, a couple of weeks of tournaments. There was swimming and sailing down on the lake, riding along sylvan bridle paths, and hiking along miles of trail. On Thursdays there were elaborate excursions with elegant picnics spread on linen cloths.

The evenings were filled with concerts by little-known musicians who performed in exchange for a rather handsome holiday (though we noted that they had the second-rate guest rooms and second-rate seating in the dining room). Following the performances there were chummy gatherings in the drawing room, where the guests played at "the game," which we came to understand meant charades.

The college kids who staffed the place had light responsibilities and lighter reimbursement. In my day, we seldom had more than five or six patrons at our tables, and often as few as two. The average weekly tip for a couple was $5. My summer's take was a disappointing $200, which didn't go far even then toward paying a year's college expenses. The food was first-class and abundant—prime rib, lamb chops, and Long Island duck were daily offerings—and what we lacked in money we made up in avoirdupois.

We were also permitted to sit out of sight on the staircase and listen to the concerts. We had free access to the tennis courts and the lake, and if you hit it off well with your patrons (as I did), sometimes they would take you on "motor trips" in their chauffeured cars, on which occasions you felt wonderfully conspicuous.

The competition was keen for the few college boys working there as bellhops or busboys or groundskeepers. I picked up a shy intellectual swain from Johns Hopkins named Jack something-or-other who mustered the courage by summer's end to ask if he could kiss me.

It was, all in all, a languorous summer of new experiences, and the memory of it grows more precious as it recedes in time. My long trip up the mountains to the Lake of the Eagles, therefore, was an eager one—to see again the Crestmont, search out the manager, introduce myself and talk of the past, inquire about old guests, buy a postcard and write to Hud and Ellie, my companions of that summer . . . :

> Dear Hud,
>
> Would you believe(!) Eaglesmere? The Crestmont still stands on its lookout high above the Lake of the Eagles (as in the picture). Alas! The tennis courts are grown over with grass and the place has a sad, abandoned look. As the guy over at the gas station said, "A hotel like that can't make it anymore on two months of business."
>
> I peered in the windows of the laundry and the old kitchen and walked down to Evergreen Lodge, where we lived, remember? Everything's there, the equipment, the furniture. Remember walking down through the pines at night, you and Ellie and me, singing old camp songs? "If there were witchcraft, I'd make two wishes . . ." I'd wish that the very rich still made their way up this hill in their chauffeured Cadillacs and that college girls still sneaked down to the dock at night to "borrow" somebody's sailboat. And then I'd wish . . . that I'd never come back to see—that they don't.
>
> Love,
> Pat

Major Purchase in Minor Key

When a farmer buys a piece of equipment from another farmer, he doesn't call him on a Tuesday morning and say, "I want to buy that combine you got for sale. What do you want for it?"

He waits until supper's out of the way, then he calls the guy, gets

his wife—"Howard around there anywhere?"—and finds out which
of his several farms Howard's working in the early evening.

Then he seeks out his own wife in the raspberry patch and says,
"Going up to see Howard. Want to ride along?"

It's not the impulsive move it sounds like, by any means. It's a
purchase they've long considered. His son has run a cost accounting
through the computer and confirmed what they already knew. The
operation can't sustain a combine profitably.

"Gonna cost us $400 more a year than if we hired it done," says
the son dejectedly. He fancies himself in the air-conditioned splendor
of one of those big green machines, waving to the neighbors as he
moves from field to field, intimidating everyone in his wake.

Dad and Mom have leaned back in the kitchen chairs, reviewing
the financial picture, considering the implications of this major purchase.

"Always take your chances with a custom combiner. He'll come
when his fields are finished, and sometimes the weather doesn't
hold."

"Like last year, for instance."

"Could lose a lot more than $400."

"Sure could."

But they don't make any vocal commitment to the purchase until
this moment when he says, "Well, if we're going up there, we'd
better get started."

Howard's over at "the home place" drying wheat. He's sitting in
his pickup chewing the fat with another guy, waiting for someone to
bring the day's last loads from the field. Even now the farmer doesn't
launch the subject of buying a combine. That would defy the rules
of sociability. He takes his social life where he can, and a satisfying
part of it gets mixed up with his business.

There's talk of the wheat harvest in progress. Howard's double-
cropping, putting soybeans on after his wheat, and the whole process
takes some discussion. They have to hash over the big square ding in
the door of the grain truck.

"Looks like the imprint of a straw spreader to me," says the
farmer.

"You got it," said Howard. "Dad thought I'd moved and I hadn't.
Saw him coming, but it was too late. Got a new door to put on there,
but didn't get to it yet." They cover last year's bean harvest, the
market prices, the rainfall, last year's rainfall, the tax bill in Congress,
and the cost of money.

"Like to take a look at that combine," says the farmer, probing finally to the subliminal business underscoring the extended conversation. They follow Howard home then down the back roads through corridors of lush field corn.

In the machinery lot out back of the farm shop the pair review the combine, dwarfed by its enormity, baffled by its green complexities, a far cry from the old Allis Chalmers 60 that was their last experience of a combine. They climb the ladders, peer into the hopper, sit in the cab, start the engine—kicking the tires, so to speak.

Some sorry farmer somewhere had thrilled to the deep rumble of this engine when it was new, paid the long price, and got in over his head. Someplace in the Midwest he is telling his friends the bitter tale of his farm auction: "They gave my combine away." This farm couple are glad that Howard through his dealings has spared them the pain of knowing the anonymous loser.

"What are you asking for it?" says the farmer at last. They discuss the terms quietly, apologetically, for money is a crass thing. It could interfere with the warmth and kinship one farmer feels for another. They strike a deal.

There'll be a time for harsher words when it throws a rod or blows a tire. But as the fireflies flicker in the soft summer twilight, Howard sees them to the car, and they talk of gentle things, of old times and family and the hopeful future. There's no telling how this purchase will end, but it begins as a neighborly encounter.

Low-Level Summit

"The Russians are coming!" my sons said excitedly, speaking of a couple of crack young motorcycle racers due in the area en route to a Grand Prix in New York State.

I've long been a sucker for a bewildered foreigner. I am the one who sheepishly reports when the intercom blares, "Would anyone speaking French please report to the information desk?" It all comes from having been so often very foreign and bewildered in another country myself.

I have also lived at great length the life of air terminals, freeways, Holiday Inns, and Burger Chefs. I have driven from our inner cities to our air terminals and recognized how ugly America is from that viewpoint. I have winced at the thought that to thousands and thousands of foreign visitors America is a mad rush of traffic flowing through fenced troughs strewn with crumpled newspapers, broken bottles, beer cans, and fast-food fallout.

America is packaged by foreign travel bureaus as a scattering of cities connected by freeways, punctuated here and there by a remarkable national park: Grand Canyon, Yosemite, Yellowstone, etc. Only those tourists who come to America to visit friends or relatives can possibly go away with any broad understanding of what life is like here.

And so I invited the Russians for dinner: Guennady (sounds like Kennedy) and Vladimir, the racers; Yuri, the supervisor assigned by the Soviet government to make sure the group returned (dubbed the "Komissar" by my kids); and Vladimir, the elder, the interpreter. The Komissar was not especially happy with the motel where they had been quartered, I was told by their American business contact:

"No restaurant in motel?"

"Next door, restaurant. Across street, restaurant."

"Not possible. Must have restaurant in motel. Pay food with motel bill."

"Why not pay for food from pocket?"

"Not system," came back from the interpreter.

But I was not intimidated by the "system." I baked some bread, fried a couple of chickens, and cooked a heap of mashed potatoes and a great platter of sweet corn, thinking it about as American as anything I could offer.

The interpreter, a dark-haired fellow of sixty, was warm and gregarious and spoke British English with a Russian accent, if such is possible.

"I do not think you have this carpet on the floor in the country," he remarked as I shook his hand and welcomed him to come in off the porch. "How do you keep it clean?"

I pointed out to him that carpeting is about the cheapest covering one can put on a floor in America. He raised his eyebrows and translated. They filed into the dining room, and I brought in the platters of food as Paul and the boys explained a bit about the farm operation. Our son Ted had shown them around the farm before lunch.

"Is all this yours?" they had asked incredulously, indicating our three-hundred-acre spread. There were questions now about the yields of our grain and potato crops and a great deal of confusion in translating bushels per acre into metric tons per hectare.

Vladimir asked Paul (who was enlarging their common vocabulary with his healthy fund of German) if it had been his father who immigrated. No, Paul explained, it was his great-grandfather who immigrated from Germany, smuggling himself away in a small boat in the night and by prearrangement climbing aboard a sailing ship outside German waters to avoid conscription under the Prussian king.

As Vladimir chuckled over that and translated it for the Komissar and the two young racers (both of whom were in the Russian army), I wondered if it stirred any longings—longings quickly dispelled by the steely eye of the grim, gray-haired Komissar, who made all the decisions for the group. Then I remembered having been told that Guennady's wife was never allowed to travel with him outside of Russia.

They were all a little hesitant about the sweet corn. (Uninitiated Europeans usually think of corn as pig food.) But they gave it a sporting try, some returning for seconds.

"*Du musst es mit Butter essen*," said Paul, passing the butter to the Komissar.

"*Kein Butter*. Too fat," he said, pushing it away and patting his ample stomach.

We dug out some slides of the farm in other seasons and brought out our collection of Indian artifacts. Foreigners are always fascinated by tangible evidence that the Red Man in America was more than a myth or a TV invention. They yearn after our lost culture as we do after theirs.

There wasn't much more to our little cultural exchange. Yuri lined everybody up in front of the house, put his camera on a tripod, and then raced to join us for the photo. As a kind of afterthought and compensation for all we hadn't been able to say to one another, I autographed a copy of one of my books "for my new friend Vladimir." His eyes shone as I pointed out my name on the cover.

He kissed my hand. I fumbled through the cheek-to-cheek ritual and hugged him. They thanked us profusely, got in their van, and went down the road. No big deal, but a warm breeze in the Cold War. What peace really demands, I am convinced, is fewer summit meetings and more subversive sweet corn and fried chicken.

Joy Is a Summer Puppy

Thatcher prostrates his little body on the stone step out front, his bare tummy in touch with the only bit of cool available to a pup on a summer day. He crosses the yard like a regal lion. He squats by the screen and howls pitifully till somebody surrenders and lets him onto the enclosed porch. He seems to recognize that for this summer, at least, he enjoys "most favored dog" status.

And small wonder! Thatcher started life in an electric skillet padded with terry cloth and set on "simmer," the sole survivor of a litter of eight blond Labs born prematurely during a spring nor'easter. Every three hours I stretched him out on a towel, pushed a tiny tube down his throat, and fed him puppy formula by syringe.

Two or three times a night I rolled from my bed and made my way down to the kitchen to see that he had not crawled from his source of warmth. When he contracted pneumonia, I put him on a heating pad under a lamp in the bathroom and ran the vaporizer until rain clouds formed and moisture dripped from the ceiling. At ten days he went on an Evenflo nursing bottle, where he continued until he could cope with puppy chow.

All the while Heidi hovered solicitously by, hanging her head over the skillet to wash him with her tongue, seeming to know that his condition was precarious and called for extraordinary measures. For short intervals she nursed him from her meager flow of milk and snarled viciously at anyone who posed a threat. It was the first time in her years at End o' Way that Heidi had been allowed indoors, and she settled comfortably into the corner of Paul's office, bringing with her the heavy odor of farm dog.

When the warm days came, Paul had had enough.

"If you don't get these dogs out of here, I'm going to have a fur ball in my throat," he growled. So with trepidation I moved my baby to the garage, certain that a rat or a coon or some other predator would do him in.

Heidi, of course, kept her vigil, leading her prize farther and farther afield each day. His pedigreed grandfather was called Winston Churchill, and because the pup survived a difficult campaign, we named him for Margaret Thatcher.

Now they grace the green lawn out front, mother and son, distracting every comer. The pup climbs on Heidi's back, sniffs in her ear, chews on her muzzle. Heidi somersaults him with her big paw, takes his small head gently in her mouth, and shakes him. At eight she is as patient as a grandmother, tolerating nonsense she never permitted with her first litter. This is her fourth and last. Perhaps she senses that. Perhaps she recognizes that Thatcher is to be the comfort of her dotage.

Thatcher passes his day in puppy antics. He guards the well stone, waiting for someone to pump him a drink. He chases his tail in circles and performs ballet maneuvers, feet suspended, ears a-flying. He nestles his plump belly among the salvia plants. He eats the petunia blossoms and chews on the fern. He rests his tail beneath the rocker on the porch and yelps pitifully when somebody rocks on it.

From the barnyard his mother charges to the rescue. He seeks comfort at her flanks in a corner of the porch. For a few moments they rest quietly, looking down the road, heads held at the same angle.

"You wanta get rid of him?" asks an old fellow who stops by for corn.

"Sure, take him along," says Orrin, "but you'll have to take my ma, too."

Dr. Elsie

There was a time in American life when people spoke of their physician by his first name preceded by the title "Doctor," transforming that name into one of love and reverence. It was a time before malpractice suits and Medicare and Blue Cross, Blue Shield. It was an era of house calls and practical remedies and pills dispensed in tiny envelopes from acrid-smelling rooms lined with shelves of generic bottles. It is an era that persists anachronistically in an obscure office down at the end of Cleveland Avenue, where Amherst thins to suburbia, where Doctor Elsie Snell pursues her holy calling next door to her big turn-of-the-century frame home.

"The thing about Doctor Elsie," says one of her loving patients, "is that people get her mixed up with God. She's been known to haul a sick patient home, put her to bed, check the refrigerator, then go out and buy groceries to sustain her." Nobody has come forth to confirm this case study, but the poor, the meek, and the neglected do not tell their stories. Doctor Elsie's charity is of the private, biblical sort, and nearly all her patients have been beneficiaries of it at one time or another.

My own satisfaction as one of those patients is that she has always been accessible, unshielded by layers of protocol, unyielding schedules, and batteries of intermediaries. An office call is casual and uncomplicated and demonstrates a respect for both your intelligence and your self-knowledge. It is a respect that proceeds from a basic understanding of you. Doctor Elsie is the only doctor who ever called unbidden to inquire after my health. She had gotten wind of the fact that I'd been treated in a hospital emergency room and wanted to be sure I was getting satisfactory care.

I'm sure she knows a malingerer from a genuinely ill patient, yet her genius is in understanding the hypochondriac in his or her real need to be listened to. "You are a *person* in Doctor Elsie's office— not a number, not the patient waiting in *A* while the nurse preps the patient in *B* and the doctor writes prescriptions for the patient in *C*!" says one of the women who has sought healing with Doctor Elsie through the years. Time to listen, freely bestowed, accounts for a large portion of Doctor Elsie's genius as a physician.

"I used to go in and stare pointedly at the clock when the waiting room was full of people and a patient had rattled on too long," said the friend who had served Doctor Elsie as nurse and office girl for twenty years. "But Doctor Elsie never complained. I think she's always felt a special kinship for the old and the lonely."

Numerous stories of her loving ministrations and of her outstanding leadership in the church and the community were exchanged when Doctor Elsie's family and friends gathered to celebrate her fifty years of medical practice. Many of them included a warm reference to her husband, Dr. C. H. Snell, who had shared the practice as well as her philosophy of service and medicine until his death in 1953.

"You folks all here to see Mama?" he used to ask as he stuck his head in the waiting room. "You're going to have a long wait. She's down at the hospital catching a baby."

Keener than her faith in medicine perhaps is Doctor Elsie's faith in God. Nobody ever went into surgery with her unsustained by prayer, and many have been comforted in their hours of agony by her strong Methodist assurance that they are not alone. Often through the years she called to cancel her office hours in order to sit quietly with a dying patient.

Now and again Doctor Elsie has considered taking in a young doctor to share the practice and assume it when she's gone. But she has had second thoughts. "I don't practice medicine like those young doctors," she says. "It probably wouldn't work."

Is Doctor Elsie's sort of casual, very human practice of medicine really impossible in today's world? Does it ask too great a sacrifice of an individual? Does it invite abuse? Should one rely more on computers and electronics and less on prayer? Perhaps. But I can't imagine bringing a malpractice suit against somebody you call "Dr. Elsie," who pauses before your child's appendectomy to ask God's blessing upon him.

Weather Watch

My husband-to-be wrote me letters during five of the nine months we courted, so I was initiated early into the ritual of the weather report. "Dear Pat," he would write, and as my heart swelled in anticipation of a tender phrase of yearning he continued, "Good news! An inch of rain yesterday."

That set the tone for the rest of the letter, a report on farm work either in progress or interrupted by rain, plus a crop forecast adjusted on the basis of that rain. Along toward the end I braced myself again for those outpourings of endearment of the sort Robert Browning wrote to Elizabeth Barrett: " . . . And so I must close for tonight and catch the weather report. Three days of sunshine and the combining will be pretty well in hand. Love, Paul."

Ah, how he loves me, I told myself, to share with me all this that is so vital. (Young girls in love are masters of self-deceit.)

I was surely right in one regard. The weather report is the preempting consideration of a farmer's life. When I married him it was with an open awareness that I would ever afterward love, honor, and watch the skies with him.

The telephone and the mail bring me frequent communications from farmers, or their wives, or sons of the soil serving agriculture in some regard. And every one of them alludes to the weather as to an important member of the family in or out of favor. No matter how good the report may seem, somehow it has disagreeable aspects.

Consider one week's offerings from around the nation·

Business conversation with a guy from Richmond, Virginia: "Got any rain up there?"

"Yeah, lots. Five inches in ten days. How's it there?"

"Dry! Terribly dry. Old fellows saying they don't ever remember a drought so bad. Everything's brown. We didn't get any first-cutting hay at all."

Jasper, Minnesota: "Nice rains up here. Our crops are fantastic. Corn shoulder high. Folks around us not so lucky. Three of my nephews had bad hail and nineteen farms were wiped out. Besides that, cutworms have been really bad. One neighbor replanted his corn three times, and at $50 a bushel for seed that's no small matter." (If you don't have your own bad news, you make do with somebody else's.)

Merrimac, Wisconsin: "Have not actually had an overabundance of rain, but enough to do a lot of good. . . . The hail didn't come as predicted. With all these good-looking beans, etc., prices will be rock-bottom low."

Warsaw, Indiana: "Thunderstorms and rain all morning. The men got so wet they came in without finishing the feeding. Bad for them to be out there in that lightning."

Erie, Pennsylvania: (Potato farmer who stopped by overnight on a travel emergency.) "All this heat and high humidity. Gotta get home and spray my spuds for blight. Stuff spreads like a son of a gun in this kind of weather."

Kent, Illinois: "Gee, it's hot! No subsoil moisture, but every so often we get a few tenths of an inch and it seems to keep us going. We're getting the jitters now because rain at tasseling time is a necessity. We keep remembering last year's drought."

Missoula, Montana: "Some spots are very dry, and some people are being forced to sell part of their herds. Hay and feed may be at a premium this winter. Rivers and creeks are running at a fraction of their normal level. If we don't have an abundance of snowfall this year we'll be in real trouble. Ranching seems to be one crisis after another."

That just about sums it up for weather—one crisis after another. If I live long enough, will I finally hear those sweet, endearing words, not those I once sought between the lines of Paul's letters, but those I now recognize and embrace as precious beyond all other words in a farmer's language: "The weather is great. The crops are terrific. The prices are out of sight!"

Well—I won't give up hope. Methuselah lived 969 years, and there are other recorded miracles. . . .

Sweet Slice of August

"When will the melons be in?" folks start asking about the middle of June, as though on some appointed day we might go down and meet them at the bus. There's an anticipation in the question that bespeaks a yearning tied to summers long ago, when a kid didn't have the Tastee Freeze and the Dairy Queen and a hundred other delights to brighten his life. You had a Popsicle or an Orange Crush and you sure as heck couldn't get either one of them out of your icebox. Maybe on Saturday night you got an ice cream cone, and it was rumored that in the cities there was a whoppin' big treat called a "banana split," but you hadn't really been that far from home. About as far as you got on an everyday basis was the muskmelon patch, so, by golly, you learned to love melon.

How I do remember it, the impatient waiting. Very early on you picked out a promising globe and kept a daily watch, riding your bike around that way, tiptoeing carefully between the vines and checking to see if there was a crack around the stem whispering, "Ripe!" Of course, that was never the melon that made it. Your brother would emerge triumphant one day with a beauty that had ripened unnoticed in a clump of weeds across the patch.

Then you'd slit 'er in wedges with the jackknife you'd been carrying all the three weeks of anticipation, carefully flick out the clinging seeds, and bury your face in the orange flesh. The older and more skillful kids would slice the meat from the rind, then cut that wedge into three or four bites, carrying each to their mouths on the point of the knife. And sitting there in the rye field behind the barn (where you wouldn't have to share your melon with too many others), elbows on your knees, juice dripping between your fingers and down the corners of your mouth, you knew the glorious fruition of summer.

When the whole patch was ripe, you got more finicky, scouting the field for a perfect melon, well netted and of just the right hue. Then you'd haul it proudly home and put it in the icebox right on top of the ice.

The crowning coup of the melon season was to hop on your bike, peddle down to the filling station with a couple of big melons, buy a pint of ice cream, then split 'em open, scoop out the seeds, and plop that ice cream right down in the middle. This was as much of a luxury as you ever had to flaunt before the motley troops who hung around the Fleet Wing station, and for as long as that rich, fruity treat lasted, and you condescended to share the wealth, you were right up there with Jack Armstrong.

Now another August, and "the melons are in." People come around to End o' Way and haul them home in hungry anticipation. A few among them ask discreetly if we have "cantaloupe." They'll pick up, shake, and smell it and punch the ends, searching for a good one, and you know that their knowledge of melons is from the grocery.

You know for sure that they never sat cross-legged in a rye field and ate an August melon, juice trickling down their arms and off their elbows.

Another Dream Fulfilled

"Here comes your new tractor," said Paul, looking up from lunch and down the road in response to the dogs' barking.

"If it's all the same to you, I'd just as soon have a Mercedes Benz," I said, looking out to where the International dealer was passing in a red blur.

The timing couldn't have been worse. I had come home late for lunch from running errands in town to find Paul cooking a couple of hot dogs (a sure sign of a farm wife's failure). As I heaved a half-bushel of canning tomatoes up onto the counter by the sink, he started carping at me about some grievances that had nothing to do with me.

"Honey, if you're angry with the guy, go tell him. Don't take it out on me!"

It evolved that the mailman had arrived just ahead of me and the implement dealer with a tardy check from the commission house. Some of the melon receipts as reflected in the check hadn't covered the cost of the boxes we packed the melons in. And now came this big new liability.

Whether I'm to hold title to "my tractor" or just pay for it had not as yet been determined, but my perambulations among farm people have taught me that a growing number of farm wives are working at outside jobs to keep the machinery from being repossessed. I pulled on my barn coat and went out to where the implement dealer had just unloaded the thing.

Shiny and red it was, and so clean! Hard to imagine this showroom model up to its axles in mud and manure. Not difficult, however, to imagine the pride of a farmer riding thereon. And a farmer's wife could cut quite a figure up there too on that adjustable, padded seat —with arms, no less. Wow!

"Well," I said sarcastically, not quite ready to surrender to this folly, "it's the right color, no doubt about that. But it doesn't have my name painted on it anyplace. And does it go with all that stuff out there that it's supposed to pull?"

A new tractor is like a new suit. The shirt and the tie, the hat and the shoes have to match—likewise, the plow, the cultivator, the front end loader, the mower, and so on. Paul assured me that this tractor would fit well into our "machinery wardrobe."

The International dealer got on it then and demonstrated how the front end loader could be simply removed by slipping the cotter pins and pulling a couple of bolts.

"There's something you should appreciate," said Paul, making veiled reference to a skirmish I once had with a tree that was camouflaged in Virginia creeper. I bent the old bucket all to heck.

" . . . and see here, Pat, it's got a Bosch carburetor—just like a Mercedes Benz," we finished in unison, laughing.

Someplace toward the end of her second or third decade as a farm wife, every woman must wake up one morning, look wistfully out toward the tractors in the machinery lot, and say to herself, "Is this all there is?"

Of course it isn't! There are new pickups, new plows, new planters, new disks; augers, manure spreaders, sprayers, chisel plows, wagons, and if you are very zealous and faithful, one golden summer day you'll get a shiny new combine!

And when Fred dies and leaves you a wealthy widow, all the eligible old duffers in the county will come around and size up your machinery lot. Just make sure it's all in your name.

Step Right Up

For the thirtieth year Paul and I have strolled the midway at the county fair, munching on peanuts and dropping the shells along the blacktop, stopping to chat with neighbors, enjoying the music of the barrel organ floating from the merry-go-round. And for the thirtieth time he has refused to turn a hand to win me a teddy bear or a Kewpie doll. (Alas for the simpering celluloid Kewpie doll, almost supplanted by accelerated generations of Disney, Schulz, and Spielberg creatures.) Maybe I met him too late—he was twenty-seven—and he didn't feel he had to prove anything by throwing basketballs through hoops ten times out of ten. He was right. We were both too old for the midway, I fear.

Ah, the pitfalls! "Shoot till you win," promises the sign above one shooting gallery where two little kids are trying their skill.

"You win, kid!" hollers the barker, handing the boy a toy of Cracker Jack proportions and shifting his own attention to the next prospect on the walk. The little fellow eyes the big stuffed animals wistfully, accepts the plastic army tank, and moves on, sadder but . . . wiser?

"We reserve the right to limit prizes," warns another booth. Imagine the swagger of a young buck who is refused his third plush tiger.

"Get outa here, kid. You're too good for this game."

"No Rebouds [*sic*]," announces one of the pitching establishments. Further on is another sign painted by the same guy: "Food Supliments." If you can't hawk the merchandise, maybe you can paint signs.

For the morbidly philosophical there is homely wisdom to be garnered on the midway. "Leaners Are Losers," it says up over the booth where you toss hoops at Pepsi bottles.

The penny arcade has become the "quarter arcade," an electronic monument to the American passion for violence. Consider the entertainment value of Attack, Shoot Out, GangBusters, Outlaw, Combat, Panzer Attack, Top Gun, Gun Fight—all rootin' tootin' cops-and-robbers and war stuff. Test your skill as a fighter pilot with Ace or Biplane, or as a submarine gunner called Sea Wolf.

Prepare for the future with Invaders from Outer Space, or grapple with Killer Shark. If you dig historical violence, there's Boot Hill, in which you shoot it out with cowboys and Indians. A quarter gives you about sixty seconds on the trigger to hone your skills in any of those combats.

The other obsession of the quarter arcade is the automobile. Drag Race is extremely popular, as is Demolition Derby. Then there's something called Junkyard, in which you work at stacking wrecked cars. Stunt Cycle is a little tamer: you play Evel Knievel and jump over autos. If you line up and jump twenty-three without wiping out more than three times, you win a free game.

But the quarter wonder that really packs 'em in is Death Race, a sadistic pursuit in which two heroes take the wheel to see who can run down the most pedestrians. When struck, the pedestrians are transformed into crosses, which line up on your side of the board. Terrific game.

The midway was always a losers' alley, but the quarter arcade vindicates it, demonstrating that even losers can be winners if you give them wheels and plenty of horsepower and, most important of all, guns.

The real winners, of course, are the silly "old" couple who saunter in holding hands, gawk around, and saunter out again. They did the whole midway for the price of a sack of peanuts.

They cut through the food concessions, stopping for a chili dog, stand in line briefly for the Ferris wheel, then soar above this glow of excitement that lights the county for one week a year. The midway at that height shrinks into perspective, a brief trail of neon that begins nowhere and fades into the summer dark.

Summer Doldrums

I don't know if it's cosmic rhythms or biorhythms or logarithms, but mid-August signals an ebb in spirits on the farm. It's a muggy afternoon and I'm heavy with woe—the bill arrived for truck repairs, the water-softener guy just fished a mouse from the salt tank, my dryer's on the fritz, the handle fell off the dishwasher, my bike has a flat tire. I go over to draw comfort from Ed, our hired man and resident "chaplain." Things get you down, take 'em to Ed. He'll clarify the issues and draft a plan for dealing with them. . . .

Ed's sitting at the kitchen table behind a glass of beer, looking not at all like the proverbial carefree and contented "man with can of beer." Rather, he is agitated.

"All I want is to see this summer end. Kiss it off! Never been a year when everything went so wrong. Tractor engine's full of sludge, combine seized up, three acres of potatoes up there drowned, farm prices at rock bottom. I don't know, man! Money going out hand over fist. Tax bill came from the IRS and I'm up there spraying, thinking how they'll pay my tax money to somebody who's sitting on a pier fishing!

"Then my brother Joe comes out here bellyaching about how the air conditioning isn't cool enough in the machine shop where he works. And my brother Andy comes over to get some sweet corn to cook on a hibachi in the locker room down at the steel mill. Fifteen bucks an hour and he's in the locker room cooking steak and corn on a hibachi! No wonder the price of cars is out of sight.

"That's another thing! I'm up at the Little League game and I look over at my car and the darned bumper's fallen off. Rusted clear through. So I've been out to the used car lots shopping for a car. Talk about depressing!"

. . . I sneaked out and left him to his beer. His problems only make my own seem more oppressive. What I need is a productive enterprise. It's canning season. I go off in search of a peck of pickles.

My pickle farmer seems to have drunk the same bitter draught. "Work our tails off! And what for? I went in the other morning to grab a bite of breakfast and I turned on the local talk show. There's this guy on there telling how he felt the consumers should get up in arms about the price of food. After what I'd been through that morning already I felt like choking the guy. Instead, I got on the phone, called the station, and told them that the American consumer has the best and the cheapest food in the world, but I don't suppose anybody really heard what I was saying. Phone call probably cost me eight bucks."

"Well, Bob," I said mischievously, sizing up the twenty-five or thirty workers milling around his packing shed, "we've got to keep these people working. Right?"

"That's just about it. We're working for the help. And the land," he added softly, looking out toward the back forty.

Home with my pickles, I discover my husband rifling through the filing cabinet. I can read the signs that tell me he's seeking a manual for a malfunctioning machine. I should know better than to start a conversation with, "Honey, my dryer's not working."

With teeth clenched and fire breathing from both nostrils he says, "I've got all the problems I can handle with the @#$%& sprayer!"

Orrin is sitting at the kitchen table with his chin in his hands. "And what's the matter with you?" I ask in exasperation.

"It's summer," he says. "I just realized that it's almost over."

And on that note I go down to the cellar to make a pickle brine that will float an egg.

Autumn

Lord, it is time. The summer was very grand.
Lay Thy shadow on the sundials,
O'er the fields loose the winds to blow.

—Rainer Maria Rilke,
"Autumn Day"

Porch Sitting

September should be devoted to sitting on the porch, looking out through the long shade to the warm place in the sun where summer was. The weeds are blossoming there now. The crabgrass is feathering, and the smartweed is a pink blush among the clover. (Frost will take the weeds and the clover will triumph.) In the fencerows the foxtail is waving. There's hardly a farmer around who appreciates the graceful sway of this noxious weed. (Though I did read once of a farmer who makes foxtail hay. Three cheers!)

It's a nice porch, tucked under the roof, quite a bit more than a stoop but yet not a veranda. Paul thought we should push out the wall and absorb the space into the kitchen, but I protested. "It belongs to the architecture, and if your great-grandmother could afford a porch, so can I."

There are tintypes in an antique cigar box here of overweight ladies in long heavy skirts, dark shawls, and bonnets, sitting, like figures in a wax museum, upon this same porch. Or is it the same? The pillars rotted away and were replaced; the floor, likewise. The clapboard has a saw curve like the original, but it is of vinyl-coated steel. God and new tenants make all things new.

The rocking chair belongs. I rescued it from the woodshed years

159

ago, sanded and painted it, and found a craftsman to weave a seat. I like to think it's the same chair those old wives sat on for the photo, though they obscured it with their bulk.

Sit on the porch and enjoy the courageous flowers. They weren't planted till July. (Three nested clay pots sit on the well stone even yet.) And they persisted through puppies and summer heat and gross neglect. We are on the same schedule, the flowers and I. Now that I have time to sit, they are ready with their flourishes.

Enjoy the fresh paint on the porch floor, the only tangible evidence of summer accomplishment. Not much, but rejoice. It involved a lot of deliberation with the guy at the hardware store. Rejoice in hardware clerks who know what they're selling, what you want to buy. "I want a blue porch paint."

"Got a nice one here—Amish Blue."

"Uhhh . . . nice, but a little dark."

"How about if I leave out one part of black? Can always add it if you don't like it." It was perfect.

"We'll call it 'Almost Amish,' " he said. "I'll mark the formula on the can."

Sit on the porch and peel apples and know that this is a timeless pursuit, linking you to three generations of Leimbach women and farm women of all time. Heidi ambles up and crowds close to me, jealous of every porch minute not devoted to her. Her wagging tail beats rhythmically on the siding, fanning mud against the white, matching the "Heidi tracks" on the blue. This is her porch, after all, and I'm invading the watchdog corner.

Sit on the porch and enjoy the smell of applesauce wafting through the open kitchen window. I bought the apples yesterday from an Amish lady down south of Apple Creek. A sign said, "Apples." And up at the end of the long driveway, in the cellar of her house set into the hill, she poured them into a sack.

The apples were disappointing, but the Amish lady was worth the price of the fruit. She was big, robust, and barefoot, with a pretty, peaceful face. She wore a white bonnet, a long burgundy pleated skirt, and a black blouse held together as is customary with straight pins. Two little carbon copies—also barefoot, long-skirted, white-bonneted—clustered about her skirts. Two older girls wandered down a path fringed with purple asters to share summer secrets in the woods. From an upstairs window yet another pair of girls gazed furtively down upon this intruder from the outside world.

She apologized for the gnarled and wormy little Melbas, "All I have left." (Her wealth lay in daughters.)

"Never mind, I'll take them." We talked then of the universal farm subject. "Did ya get some rain?"

"Nice rain. Needed it."

"Sure did." I turned my car around on the steep hillside and drove off, curving past the front porch.

It was not Amish Blue, nor much sat upon, I judged. But I had relieved her of those apples. Maybe today she too sits on her porch, watching the butterflies sip nectar from the purple asters.

Vigil

Our son is alone tonight in a crowd of nurses, doctors, technicians, loving aunts, uncles, cousins, friends, and family—sustained by a network of tubes and tanks, gauges and gauze, pins and pulleys, polyester, plastic, rubber, and stainless steel.

Through the cords of the traction apparatus the clock on the wall says 2:00 a.m. I hold his unresponsive hand, study his swollen face where only his beautiful eyebrows seem to be his own, and think on other 2:00 a.m.'s.

. . . Time for the two o'clock feeding. I cradle him in my arms and quiet his hungry cries. Feedings often stretched till four as I became engrossed in a book. Teddy and I and *Dr. Zhivago* alone in the night in the cozy warmth of the upstairs bathroom.

Ted was not our first son, born untimely to insecure routines and insecure parents, but our second, the wonder child of eight years' longing. We painted the nursery pink, relined the old spool cradle. (There were latent longings for a girl, which we soon outgrew.) Grandma Penton carded wool for a tiny comforter covered in pink-and-blue plaid. I put a frilly lamp there beside the antique walnut bed, and during the restless nights in the weeks before his birth, I would read by the soft light, look over into the cradle, and dream of the child who would be Teddy. . . .

Sunday's child, born the day after Valentine's Day, a strong, healthy baby. A little boy with an elfin face, serious and humorless, slightly pigeon-toed, pushing a tractor in a sandpile, discovering he had a "motor"—Bbbrrrr. . . ." A shy child going timorously to school with new crayons tucked in a red barn lunch box.

A small farmer coming home from third grade to back potato wagons into the barn while the adult help looked sheepishly on. A broken arm, a hurried trip to the hospital, and loud wails of, "Oooo, now I can't grow up!"

A cocky little second baseman in a felt cap and a black Brownhelm T-shirt. An early morning fisherman at the back door with a bass for an unenthusiastic mother. A 4-H-er with a pen of Hampshire white pigs and a duck named George. A skinny kid with a butch haircut and a plaid windbreaker standing by the bell post waiting for the school bus and the adventure of junior high.

And then, on any Sunday, a gung-ho minibike racer, and on every Sunday evening table, a trophy for a centerpiece.

And each year another two or three inches penciled on the end of the white bookcase, Ted's marks always a little higher than those of his brothers. Each year, a little shorter on shyness and insecurity.

Ted the party boy, with girls on the phone saying, "Tell him to call back."

"Tell them I don't make house calls."

Ted "blowing them all in the weeds" at the motorcycle trials, taking on the nonchalance of the sports hero, pictures in magazines, checks from the manufacturers.

Hail-fellow-well-met, Joe College-of-Agriculture, coming home with innovative ideas from ag econ.

"Prof says the look of the place is crucial. First thing we gotta do is tear down those old barns, get you a big office and a computer."

And then on Thursday last, running an errand for his mom in a rainstorm, his car hit head-on with a truck—center line between life and death, head-on with his God, our Teddy struggles alone.

Requiem

When Ted was a lad and you asked him the "when you grow up" question, he'd say, "I'm going to race motorcycles till I'm too old, and then I'm going to farm." In a somewhat complicated way he managed to pursue those dual goals.

During the winter and spring quarters of his junior year at Ohio State he flew on successive weekends to Georgia, Michigan, California, Virginia, Oklahoma, Oregon, Washington, and Alabama to race. During the week, he grappled with agronomy, marketing, and ag economics. All summer he would mow and cultivate, pick and pack until four o'clock, then go off to work on a motorcycle engine till after midnight. The culmination of all this winter, spring, and summer endeavor was to be the International Six Day Race in France in September.

This is a long grueling race threaded through mountains and valleys, riverbeds and fire trails, thickets and meadows. The riders depart four to a minute at 7:00 each morning and cover 200 or more miles each day. If a rider can maintain a constant pace, keep his machine together, and stay on the mandated schedule for all of the six days he earns a gold medal.

Ted was bent on his third gold. He had run four months of qualifying races, earned a spot on the American team, and been assigned a number and a departure time, or "key time," for the opening day of the race. He had his plane ticket, his cycle in a crate, and his gear in the duffles when he was critically injured in an automobile accident September 4. For two and a half weeks he lay in an intensive-care ward in a more or less comatose state. With hearts heavier than their cycles or their gear, Ted's brother and his comrades flew off to France without him.

At 2:45 a.m. on the first day of the Six Days Teddy burst an artery in his chest; the doctor and nurses were at a loss to explain this serious and unexpected complication. But they didn't know our Ted, his total concentration on his singular passion. Ted was to have been off the line at 8:08 that morning. When he exerted the strain that burst his damaged artery, it was 2:45 a.m. in Ohio but in the south of France it was 8:45. Coincidence, perhaps. But no one speaks with certainty about the workings of the subconscious mind.

On the morning that would have marked the first of his senior year as an ag student at O.S.U. Ted's artery hemorrhaged again, too much this time for the once-powerful body.

The nights turned cool and the leaves changed color. South of the lane where the land slopes toward the river, Teddy's soybeans ripened in the late September afternoon. The motorcycle trails to the lower flats were strewn with early-fallen leaves. Somewhere in the south of France the medals were awarded. On that day our son vanished into the green-gold paradise that had nurtured him. Nobody who knew him doubts that Teddy got his "gold."

Compensation

On a scale of one to ten, Courtney's first birthday party was an unqualified ten. There were the requisite number of little cousins, wiser in the ways of birthdays than the birthday girl herself, shivering in anticipation. There were the anxious aunts trying to keep their toddlers off the end tables and out of the flowerbeds, scraping food from the carpet pile with table knives, and rushing two-year-olds to the bathroom. There were uncles going back for seconds on baked beans and potato salad, gurgling and cooing and tossing little children into the air.

There were proud grandparents with gifts more lavish than they had bought Courtney's parents twenty-eight years ago, grateful that they could depart this hubbub and go home to an atmosphere of order.

There was promise of future birthday parties in the watermelon lumps under the tunic shirts of the pretty slim mommies. There was the Reverend Peter William VanderWyden III making a desperate effort to be unflappable about Peter William VanderWyden IV dragging on the nursing bottle of the guest of honor. And of course there were the great-aunts beaming on all the proceedings, a little indignant at being great-aunts a whole generation before they were great-grandmothers.

There was a bustling mama and a camera-snapping papa and a totally unconcerned, nonchalant Courtney swathed in a cross-stitched bib, mashing chocolate cake with sticky fists into eyes and ears and hair and mouth, then grasping for an adjacent philodendron.

There were the predictable climaxes—the darkened room, the cake with single candle, the camera floodlights, the discordant singing, and all the cousins blowing through wide-set teeth, then the five-year-old with the coup de grace to extinguish the flame, and the mirthful applause.

Finally there were the presents in the living room, Courtney stomping happily on the two-dollar wrap job of the godmother, each little cousin clamoring to unwrap the present he had brought, "no-no-ing" mothers trying to reenforce the manners of the culture. Then the oohing and the ahing and the bedlam of children squabbling over the same pull toy. Happy, happy clamor, not unlike birthday celebrations of the seventies, the sixties, the fifties, and the forties that the great-aunts were party to.

There were, however, several marks of the eighties. The little girls frolicked about in Calvin Klein jeans. Six-dollar Brownie box cameras had given way to $300 marvels from Germany and Japan. Grandpa came with his new wife and shook hands amiably with Grandma's new husband, and Courtney made a haul probably worth a cool two hundred bucks.

But there was a special joy about Courtney's birthday party not to be captured by a Nikon, a Leica, or a Polaroid Land camera. Two years earlier the Reverend VanderWyden had gathered with this same concerned assemblage around a tiny grave and delivered a eulogy for the firstborn child of today's rejoicing parents.

The Prophet said, "[Joy and Sorrow] are inseparable. Together they come, and when one sits alone with you at your board, remember that the other is asleep upon your bed" (Kahlil Gibran, *The Prophet*).

Aunt Pat and Uncle Paul took it all as a hopeful sign.

At Liberty

When the cicadas begin their trilling and the night music is of crickets and tree toads, the men of my household begin thinking "sweet pickles."

"Only one jar left down in the cellar. Isn't this the year to do pickles?" (They're such an involved process that I only do them biennially.)

Locating a fresh pickle source is sometimes a trick, but Paul has his contacts, and on some unscheduled day a couple of pecks will appear on the kitchen counter. The liberation of women, however, has made inroads on many time-hallowed traditions, and pickle making is not exempt.

"You fellows are going to have to finish these pickles," said I one night as I made my lists, sorted the laundry, and packed my gear for a four-day absence. "Tomorrow, drain off the alum water, wash the pickles, then heat this syrup and pour it over. Every morning for the next four days, drain the syrup, reheat it, and pour it over the pickles."

"Why can't we just heat the whole business, pickles and all?" asks Paul.

"I don't know. The recipe says 'drain the syrup, heat, and pour over the pickles.' "

"But if the syrup's boiling, doesn't it have the same effect as heating the pickles with the syrup?" chimes in Orrin.

"Look, this was my great-grandmother's recipe, and that's the way she did it. So that's the way I do it. I don't know why she did it that way, but I'm sure she had a reason."

"Doesn't make a darned bit of sense," persists Paul.

"Well, I'm leaving, and you're free to make the pickles any old way you want. The recipe's propped up over there against the crock. But don't forget! I've already got two weeks' time and $8.50 invested in that crock of pickles!"

He's going to change my great-grandmother's pickle recipe, I just know it. This guy, who wouldn't make a U-turn on a freeway to save himself 300 miles of travel; this good citizen who waits for traffic lights in the middle of nowhere in the middle of the night; this man who is so law-abiding that he will not rip a "do-not-remove" tag from a ten-year-old mattress!

Given the freedom to run the house as he chooses while I pursue subsidiary careers as writer and public speaker, this fellow is going to tamper with something as venerable as his great-grandmother-in-law's pickle recipe.

Did Betty Friedan have any idea what she was unleashing when she launched this movement? Equal rights is one thing, but when it penetrates to Grandma's pickles, well, that's shaking the foundations!

Ground Cover

Out front, under the ninety-year-old maples that Paul's granddad planted as a young man, I will a lawn. "Let there be grass," I say, but there is no grass. When I was young and filled with hope, I hauled in topsoil and raked and seeded and rolled. The straw I spread there promptly blew away. The dogs wandered across and nestled into the dusty softness of it. The children rode their trikes across or dragged out little tractors and miniature equipment and "farmed" up a storm.

Other years I repeated the process with water and fertilizer. Once I fenced it all with stakes and rope that the kids and the dogs, like the wind, ignored. I took a whirl at planting myrtle out there. "Great for shaded areas," somebody said. They'd never read the statistics on the water consumed by three forty-foot maples. Another season I tried pachysandra. "Terrific ground cover for shade," said another groundskeeper. Pachysandra does not flourish on a shaded desert, I now testify.

Finally I did the only sensible thing to be done where maples crowd a house foundation. I planted brick. (Well, I hauled in the brick and made heroic overtures, and Paul laid out a patio.) Still there is an irregular area where the roots heave that defies the symmetry of brick.

Only in the autumn, when the rain of golden leaves begins, do I take pleasure in that half-acre of not-quite lawn. It's a pleasure that mounts with the accumulating mass. I love to kick them along the brick path to the mailbox and then look back at my beloved century house, its red front door standing out gaily above the puddle of gold that floods the front yard. I could pretend there's a green lawn under there, but somehow knowing it's hard, parched earth that gave up its moisture to produce this splendid cover is more compensating to the spirit.

Grousing about one's leaf problems belongs to the national obsession with lawn care. Along the curbs are rows of plastic sacks stuffed with leaves. Here and there a leafy lawn stands out amid unnatural autumn rectangles of green, and I sense the unrest in a neighborhood. It's un-American not to rake your leaves, to let them drift carelessly onto your neighbor's Chem-lawned showplace.

But me, I look out at my blanket of leaves turning from gold to peachy brown, and I am altogether content. They blow in under the barberry bushes, insulate the foundation, and undergird the evergreens. My dog curls herself into the crisp warmth of them and dreams of rabbits and woodchucks.

Some brisk November day the wind will sweep down the long, open mile between here and the Walkers' up on Gore-Orphanage Road and whoosh the leaves away, beyond the house, beyond the river valley, beyond the fall and summer that were. One of the nicest features of End o' Way is that the Lord lends a hand with the yard work.

Gone Fishin'

Brother Ted called me from a hospital bed on a hectic summer morning to deliver one of his classic homilies. "Back in the late thirties when I was courting Mabel," said he, "I made a lot of trips out to Paulding County in that old '29 Plymouth I had. And I got pretty familiar with the gas stations along the way. I remember one time stopping at a station in Napoleon where I knew the guy pretty well. He came out of his garage after a bit, wiping his hands on a grease rag.

" 'I guess you got a lot of work,' I said to him.

" 'Yup. A fellow could get too busy,' he said. 'Forget to go fishin' or visit his friends when they're sick.'

"I never forgot those words," said Ted.

And Ted's friends will testify that he never did. He's never been too busy to "go fishin' " or visit his sick friends. I remember his once entreating someone to go visit a wino they both knew who was ill and abandoned. "Hey, if you're near the hospital, stop and see the poor old devil."

I took Ted's sermon as the reproof it was, and that week I went fishing, after a manner of speaking, and visited my sick friends. I went to see Ted where he convalesced on his porch, studying the Bible with my sister-in-law Mabel.

And I went to the rest home to see my dear friend Jim. Some good angel had come to play the piano in the lounge and provide a sing-along for young hearts in worn bodies. Singing, "Darling, I am growing old . . . Life is fading fast away," in the company of forlorn old ladies in wheelchairs will tear your heart out.

Then I went to the Methodist Home to sit at suppertime with Martha Taft, who would like more than anything "to go home" to the Ridge, where she and Fred were so happy with their gardening. She wonders "what the Lord will have for us to do on the other side . . .?"

Finally I visited Mary Dolliver (Dean Emeritus of Oberlin College), warm, loving, appreciative spirit as always, who brightened at my tale of the sing-along and sang me a couple of old Methodist camp songs that were her stock-in-trade when she too played the piano for the heart's lifting (for the servicemen overseas during World War II).

As for "fishin' "—well, I rode my bike around the neighborhood, stopping for coffee with friends I don't see often. One afternoon I abandoned the lima bean patch and walked back to "the point," a mossy clearing above the river's bend where a thin point of shale stands stubbornly against the stream's meanderings. It was a favorite haunt of all the children in their discovery years. They went there to camp, to fish, to hide, to play Indians and scouts. It was such a wondrous place that they insisted Mom "come and see. . . ." I remember their scampering up and down the bank there like squirrels.

I sat on the breezy promontory and shed a few tears for those children who are no more. Then nostalgia led me along the trail at valley's edge in search of "the carving tree," on whose silvery bark three or four generations of Rugby children have memorialized themselves. It was overgrown now with brambles and saplings and blocked at one place by a fallen treetop. I was moved to climb over even that, though progress became increasingly difficult. Beyond the maze of tangled limbs, however, I found the huge beech, and sure enough, high above the other carvings and distinct from them I found what I had never seen but suspected would be there, the legacy of one of those little boys of long ago, our late son, "TED L. NO. 1—living testimony to the fact that youth is not always wasted on the young, an affirmation of his Uncle Ted's basic philosophy: there is only *this* day to live—no more.

Next to Godliness

Paul and I go to the church Saturday night to fill in for the ailing janitor. Paul does the holy dusting, I the holy vacuuming. There are lots of monotonous, unlittered miles of vacuuming in a church. "You don't have to do all that," says Paul.

"God would know," says I, "and Hazel Northeim." (This is Hazel's pew. I give it an extra pass.) Nearly everybody has his own pew in a small church. There's no name there, just an understanding. The same folks always come early, claim the rear pews. This is mine —left front. I hear well up here and there's no stampede to take it from me, except on Easter. I pick up embroidery threads from my last Sunday's holy stitching.

In the choir loft are a few dead wasps and a holy flyswatter. Ralph Leimbach was on wasp maneuvers last week during the Doxology, sopranos tittering. Nice to have something to sweep up at last.

Paul is now finished dusting pews, removing old bulletins from hymnals, and turning the books so their cover crosses are upright. The windowsills, baseboards, altar, and pulpits have passed the white glove test, and he has gone in search of Windex for the small panes on the front door. He sees window smudges through his mother's eyes. Atavism. I see only the fading light.

We move then downstairs to the "parish hall," which used to be the church basement before we hung drapes and got uppity. It's my first look at the new drapes. Impeccable taste, but a bit tame for me. There's to be a coffee klatch after church tomorrow for the missionary education committee. Somebody will say, "Aren't the drapes lovely?" and I'll say, "Yes." (Holy hypocrisy.)

Paul pushes the broad dust mop and I move into the new wing. As I clean the parlor, I'm remembering this church as it was when I came here—a kitchen without running water, and a holy privy.

Will God or Mabel Reinhard notice if I don't clean the nursery? Neat as a pin—like Mabel. Thirty years of missing sermons to dry the tears of the parish toddlers in a makeshift nursery in that drafty kitchen! Now she has this gay, sunny, warm room with a plaid shag rug.

The preacher's study is the last room to be swept. Pleasant in here with accents of orange, African artifacts, a drawing from Paul Klee. All those pastors who dreamed of a study at the church, where are they now? Did they ever get their studies?

We empty the wastebaskets, bundle the cleaning rags, turn out the lights, and climb the stairs to the sanctuary, serene and simple, absolved now of its dirt. The last, long rays of the November sun catch the stained glass and cast tints of green and gold upon the chancel and its appointments, memorial gifts all—Jane Dunnewold's quilted wall hanging of the Creation, Doris Bechtel's brass cross, Vic Schnaak's candelabra, Ed Whitmore's flag, Bob Kneisel's piano. These premises are alive in this evening hour with the memory of the good people who have worshiped here. We extinguish the last light, latch the door behind us, and beyond the shining windows the faithful saints keep watch.

Harvest Home

Yesterday in a cold drizzle I went out with my camera to photograph the gingko in its final golden glory. Last night the temperature-dropped to twenty-eight degrees, and this morning the gingko leaves look like Little Black Sambo's tigers melted to "butter" beneath the tree.

Yesterday too the coal man came with two tons of good anthracite —big, solid lumps of stuff I may have trouble balancing on a coal shovel. It will surely hold the fire through the long blizzardy nights to come. I set to rise a batch of whole wheat bread so "naturally" nutritious it could start alfalfa sprouts in your ears. (For want of one of those expensive home flour mills, I've discovered I can crack my own wheat in the blender. Makes for good chewing in the moist, heavy bread.)

In an afternoon burst of ambition I took down the curtains, washed, and starched them. While I scrubbed the woodwork, Paul ironed the curtains and rehung them, the aroma of fresh bread filling the house.

So today I can sit at my counter, look out at the first snow flurries through gleaming windows, and count my blessings, pausing at intervals to stoke the wood stove. No matter what the calendar says, the first really cold day in November is always my personal Thanksgiving.

Brown bread, black anthracite, gleaming windows, and the memory of golden trees are a lot to be thankful for, but not nearly all: I'm glad to have more work to do than I can accomplish in a lifetime. We are disturbingly aware here in the "rust belt" of the many ambitious young people who are without steady work.

I'm grateful for the abundant yield that fills the barn and the grain bin, overflowing into a new machinery shed. Rain that comes right after harvest, ending a long dry summer and providing a final burst of green lawn, is cause for rejoicing. The extended warmth of autumn was a bonus to compensate for sagging markets and spirits weighed heavily with personal woe.

Praise the Lord that the election is past, with its acrimony and antagonism flagged by frustrations, political and economic. I wish the winners well and pray the challenge of their jobs will make them greater, not lesser, mortals.

This sturdy old house with its warmth, its cheerful colors, and its momentary order figures strongly in the well-being of this day. The fact that its history and personality are ours lends continuity to our lives, as does the land and the promise of growing years to come. Down in the cellar the freezer and the old can cupboards are a cornucopia of summer's goodness.

Orrin called last evening from the university to talk with his dad about a paper he's writing on insects in potatoes. The fact that he shares our enthusiasms and our hopes for the future figures in our thanksgiving.

To be warm and well, blessed with fruitful employ and fruitful prospects—is that what it is to be thankful? Do we only know thanksgiving as a condition that separates us from those more meagerly blessed?

When the weatherman announces "the coldest recorded temperature for this date, eighteen degrees back in 1951," Paul supplies still another reason for gratitude today.

"Remember *that* fall—when Dane was a baby? We put his bassinet in the back seat of the car up in the field while Dad and Mom and you and I grubbed away at the potatoes . . . ?"

Well do I remember—the cold and the mud, the helplessness of our struggling there alone in the freezing rain, the panic of seeing the darkness gather, knowing we would have to abandon the acres that were left. . . . There is another dimension to thankfulness: the awareness of where one is compared with where one has been; the conviction that one can survive overwhelming hardship and loss.

It is not naivete or unworldliness that makes religion a stronger force among rural people. It is the elemental nature of our dependence, our rewards; the continuity of generations involved with those same elemental forces, often—as in our case—on the same land, beneath the same roof. Thanksgiving wells up as an instinctive response, religion or no.

Worthy News

The *Pike Press* of Pike County, Illinois, is printed on Wednesday and is in the hands of the citizenry the following morning. I arrived in Pittsfield, Illinois, on Thursday morning, went to lunch with three of the local matrons, and found myself caught up in the scuttlebut.

Everybody in Pike County reads the *Pike Press*. Even beyond the grave they read the *Pike Press*: "Four years have passed since that sad day when one we loved was called away. You are not forgotten, loved one, nor will you be. . . ." By late afternoon I too was reading the *Pike Press*.

This week's lead article told of a petition carried to the town council protesting the prevalence of R-rated movies. A fellow named Gates, who runs the Zoe theater, protested that he'd have to shut down if he didn't run R-rated movies, and the council tabled the matter.

Christmas and church bazaars were big news this week, but the true grit in the *Pike Press* is the fodder from the stringers around the county, who, it would appear, get paid by the inch: "Quite a few folks in New Canton have had the flu." High point of the week in Pearl was the golden wedding of the Harry Joneses in the church basement Sunday. "Mrs. Eddie Eppenheimer, daughter of Betty Lewis, baked the tiered cake."

In Fairmont, we read, "Mrs. Sonny Whitmore and children spent Saturday evening with Mr. and Mrs. Eldred Whitmore while Sonny went coon hunting." The Pittsfield lowdown appears in a column called "Here and There with Edith." We learn who had lunch at the Bobby Joe Womble home on Thanksgiving, that "Dale Black's home has not been sold and will not be till their future home is in readiness," and "When Mr. and Mrs. J. M. Sapp took Ira Tedrow to consult his doctor in Peoria he got a good report and doesn't return to the doctor till December 20. Ira is able to attend church and go to the post office."

The news is not good from Kinderhook. Lowell Lewton's father was struck on the highway crossing to the barn "where he kept a few hogs." The same week the hired man "became entangled in some farm machinery and was painfully injured."

There are surprising services offered in the *Pike Press*: Mike Niebur, the friendly undertaker, recommends that you stop by "to plan your own funeral."

You begin to understand why farm boys these days are having trouble finding wives: "Surprise your wife for Christmas," reads the Johnson Implement ad. "Give yourself and her that new four-wheel-drive diesel tractor you've been wanting." Or perhaps you might like to surprise her with an "extra good" hog shed or a registered boar: "Zimmerman Hampshires are back in business again since the fire," you discover in the classified. Old Zim must work both sides of the street. Under AUTOMOTIVE he announces, "Another Big Cheapie.

When we say Big, we mean Big. This baby uses gas! So what? You can buy lots of gas with big savings. Books at $275. Will sell for $250."

If you read between the lines in the classified, you get a little of the news that was overlooked: "Harold Slight needs driver's license and hunting license from lost wallet to complete insurance claim on accident Saturday (slight accident)."

Under MISCELLANEOUS: "Absolutely no hunting or trespassing, day or night. Myron Campbell, Baylis."

Across the page in LOST something caught my dog-loving eye: "Male Australian Blue Heeler, name of Skip. Lost around Baylis." (Sonny Whitmore's coon dog, maybe? Check with Myron Campbell.)

From WANTED, an intriguing ad jumped right out at me—help, perhaps, for the brow-beaten farm wife: "Ladies' answer to financial security. $205.80 GUARANTEED for five-hour workweek at home." No further description, no prior work experience called for, no references required. That's a tidy sum that would cover the payments on that four-wheel-drive diesel surprise, or perhaps buy her that Heap Big Cheapie.

The small-town weekly is, in effect, the glue that holds a community together. Nothing earth shattering there. Just a lot of chatter for sophisticated folks to poke fun at in distant suburbs. Just the most important paper in the world to the folks in Pittsfield and Fairmont and Kinderhook, because it tells them what they cannot find in the *New York Times* and the *Washington Post* and the *Wall Street Journal*— that they matter. Just ask Ira Tedrow.

Winter

O Wind,
If Winter come, can Spring be far behind?

—Percy Bysshe Shelley,
"Ode to the West Wind"

Bazaar

I am up very late sewing a calico cat for the church bazaar tomorrow. Ridiculous business, a calico cat . . . and a church bazaar.

We long ago made a judgment about such things at Brownhelm Church: that if people didn't believe strongly enough in the ministry of the church to support it with their offerings, then it wasn't worth preserving. With that, we abandoned the laborious chicken suppers that seemed to consume the month of July. And lo, the timbers sustained the roof, and the pledges upheld the program.

Yet . . . some kind of spirit went with the suppers, a spirit born of phoning people and riding to the church with them to set tables or brown chicken or arrange flowers; of gathering in someone's back yard to cut slaw or working frantically in the heat of the dinner hour; of sagging down at day's end to eat the leavings and count the money, then rising wearily to clean up the mess; of crawling home by moonlight, mulling over the silly laughter, the inside jokes, the friendly insults calculated to put someone at ease, some confidence shared with an old friend, some revelation about the "new people" in church you'd never known quite what to say to after services on Sunday mornings.

So somebody who missed all that, or perhaps had never known it, dreamed up a church bazaar.

Everybody else is doing it. Why not Brownhelm Church? Country and crafts are very "in," and shucks, we were country when country wasn't cool. But does the world really need another church bazaar? No, but maybe *we* need a church bazaar.

Yes, I must get the tail on this cat, weight it with sand, tie a ribbon around its neck. Very nice, this cat of blue calico. I'd really like to keep it—and that's the test, but not the idea. I must assign it a price. Seven dollars is about what I'd like to pay for a handsome doorstop. At $10 I'd probably "think about it" awhile. In point of fact, it cost me three bucks and two hours of my time. At $7, that's $2 an hour for labor. Well, that's how it is with fancy work and a church bazaar.

One of the great bargains of every church bazaar is a pot holder tightly crocheted of heavy cotton thread that took some little old lady three hours and a dollar's worth of crochet cotton. My kitchen drawer is full of them, and I never paid more than $2. Who do I think I am with this useless cat? Ten dollars indeed!

Perhaps I could write him up a pedigree and sell him for $34. . . .

"This is to certify that this Potato Patch Cat was delivered by me, Pat Leimbach, and is unique among cats of the species calico.

NAME: Katzen Jammer.

BIRTHPLACE: End o' Way Farm in the heat of midnight, October 12, 1984.

SIRED: Of Christian Zeal out of Flagging Spirit.

CARE: Minimal. Do not feed or water. Sandbox internalized. Prime pet." Ah, yes. . . .

And tomorrow I shall carry him to the church bazaar to sell to some other church member who spent two hours of her time making noodles, which I shall buy for $1.50 a pound.

Bizarre indeed, what we do for the glory of God.

Joy to the World

It came to pass on Hanukkah that our son and his wife, who was great with child, went up from their house on Kraft Street in Grand Rapids, Michigan, even unto Butterworth Hospital, for their obstetrician was of the staff of that institution. And the days were accomplished that she should be delivered, and our son stood by in a wrinkled green gown and mask and timed her contractions after the teachings of the Lamaze class, as is the custom in these latter days. And she brought forth a daughter, and they wrapped her in Health-Tex togs and laid her in a sterile crib in a climate-controlled nursery, because inns these days are not considered fit places for such miracles.

And there were in another "country" grandparents abiding, keeping watch over their midnight sheep, and an angel of Ma Bell rang unto them and they were sore afraid, for calls in the night have not always been portents of great joy. And their son spake unto them, saying, "Fear not, for unto you is born this night in the city of Grand Rapids a granddaughter, and her name shall be called Sarah Caldwell, because she is of the house and lineage of Caldwell."

And suddenly there was with our son on the telephone our daughter-in-law, saying "Yea! She is a girl! And she weigheth five pounds and eleven ounces, and she hath a sheaf of dark hair." And our son saith unto us, "Thou knowest that I am of a great objectivity in these matters, and babies generally are like unto small apes, but verily, this one is really cute! And this shall be a sign unto you, we shall bring your grandchild unto the house of her grandparents, even unto Ohio, when the Christmastide is upon us."

And grandmother spake unto grandmother, saying, "Let us now go even unto Grand Rapids and see this thing which is come to pass, which our son and daughter have made known unto us!" But grandfathers spake unto grandmothers, and they were sore restrained.

And when eleven days were accomplished, the parents brought the child to Ohio to present her to her grandparents, and when they had seen it, the grandparents made known abroad the saying which their son had told them concerning the child, "Verily, our son spake the truth. *This* one really is cute!"

And there came aunts and uncles and cousins from the east and the west, the north and the south, gazing upon Sarah Caldwell Leimbach, verifying all that which had been said of her by her father and reiterated by her grandparents.

Now when Christmas Eve came, they wrapped Sarah in the woolens of her great-grandmother and carried her to the "temple," where she slept a blessed sleep as the multitudes called up a silent night, a stable rude, a star, and a Madonna with the baby Jesus. And for the attendant relatives that night Sarah Caldwell was the incarnation of the Christ child, the fulfillment of a long dream—as perfect a miracle as any luminary in the heavens.

And the Christmas season passed in joy and wonderment. The glory of Sarah Caldwell Leimbach shone about them, and nobody doubted that her name should be called "Wonderful!"

Snow "Ball"

The snow fell silently as tears through the still night, and on January 1 there was a new world to go with the new day and the new year. I knew it when I opened my eyes with the first light to see the maple branches supporting their white burden against the gray sky.

I slipped out of bed, dressed, and went to the kitchen, where I became too soon embroiled in the holiday routines: poke up the furnace, light the fireplace, brown the spareribs, set the rolls to rising, put the leaves in the table. . . .

Dinner filled the intermission between the Cotton Bowl and the Rose Bowl. By the time the relatives had laid waste the feast, it was a quarter to four, and I'd only been out of the house to feed the dogs.

"I want to take a walk," I said, almost indignantly. "Who wants to go?" To my surprise I got seven out of twelve of the celebrants. Aunt Mary volunteered to clean up the kitchen. The gladiator watchers were staking claim to the couches as we collected boots and parkas, cameras and mittens, and set off for the woods.

Every branch and bush and bucket wore a clean white hood. Every discordant object was harmonized in snow. Even the trash pile behind the horse barn had a shrouded dignity. Orrin set up his tripod to capture the barns in their frosted aspect, as his sister-in-law Karen framed a picture through a segment of hollow log, remnant of an autumn wood-chopping session. It was a different scene, and we were immediately different people, giddy and unreserved.

"C'mon, you guys," called my niece Sylvia, "take a picture of us." We clustered against the embankment to the barn. Orrin adjusted the tripod, set the camera switch, and ran to join us for one of those goofy group shots to be duly labeled in the album, "Aunt Pat's— New Year's Day—1981."

Then we started downhill, nephew Tim in the lead leaping, waving his arms, rolling for some distance in the snow, then up and running again. "Let's do wild things," he called jubilantly, trying to convey to his proper aunts and cousins that an unconventional outing called for unconventional behavior.

Down then to the pond, where we gingerly violated the smooth snow blanket, making big slushy tracks to the far side. We followed the valley rim, and I pointed out the forty-foot pine trees, explaining that Paul had planted them about the time we were married. "My father-in-law and I cut eight or ten cedar trees right along here the day Paul and I were married. Decorated the church chancel with them."

The photographers lingered over their still lifes while the rest of us plowed on, remarking over and over at the spectacular scenes. "Look at this! And this . . . and this!"

I dared not hope that I could lure them to the river. It was such a long walk down. But beauty has a way with folks that reason cannot deter. Down the dugway we went, led by some invisible piper. We lost sight of the uplands in the long steep tunnel of snow-covered trees.

"Those guys are so busy photographing they can't see the scenery," said Aunt Donna. "Do you think we'll be able to hold the memory of all this splendor?"

"We won't have to. We'll have their pictures," I said. We all laughed then as we waited for Orrin and his sister-in-law.

For a mile or so we navigated the river, picking our way around the open water over the rapids, the more timid hanging back to see who would be first to break the ice.

"If you start to fall through, spread your arms. Create all the surface you can," said Orrin in Scout-manual mimicry. (Nowhere was the water more than a couple of feet deep.) "There's Mom's rock," he said, indicating a broad flat boulder where I had dreamed away some long-ago summer afternoons.

We all crawled up on the rock to be photographed for posterity, then made our way upriver toward the Indian fort. The slightest nudge to a sapling brought delightful snow showers. Tim struck a pose, and Karen snapped him as the snow cascaded around his ears.

Following an arduous hour of crisscrossing the river, skirting the rapids, scrambling over fallen logs, and tramping down reedy underbrush, we picked up an old logging trail that led uphill past the mossy bluff where we picnic in summer.

"Scenic overlook! Everybody gather." We looked down to the river whence we'd climbed, and nobody complained of the effort as I had anticipated.

"I could give you a push and lose a cousin," said Kelly to Tim.

"But I'm gonna hang on, so we're not gonna do it, are we," said Tim, grabbing her playfully.

Then we were out of the woods, at the foot of the sloping fields that lead back to the house.

Darkness was coming on as we straggled single file across the open field, subdued now in happy exhaustion, each with his own thoughts —held in the soft white silence.

The snow began once more, falling silently as tears. . . .

Backwater

On a snowy, blowy day in February I made a precarious trip to Fort Wayne, Indiana, only to find that the Farmers' Union meeting I was to speak for had been postponed. I was placed on twenty-four-hour hold and gained for myself a day of renewal the likes of which my recent winters have held too few.

I was bunked in the spare bedroom of Ron and Jane Hockemeyer, who dairy farm with Ron's folks along the Maumee River east of Fort Wayne.

I awakened at eight o'clock (having missed the morning milking) to a country breakfast of the sort the cholesterol mongers have nearly eliminated—hot cinnamon buns and slab bacon with eggs fried sunny-side-up in the drippings.

To keep the blood circulating and justify my intrusion on the Hockemeyers, I mixed up a batch of bread after breakfast and settled myself in a corner of the living room sofa to read a bell-ringer of a book (*Dandelion Wine*, by Ray Bradbury). Pretty Jane Hockemeyer sat in a rocker in the morning sun, a blue-jeaned Madonna nursing her baby.

At eleven o'clock Grandpa Hockemeyer, in coveralls and earlap cap and six-buckle arctics, shoveled his way in to get a reassuring peek at his wee grandson and bring the "lady speaker" a copy of the *Drovers' Journal*. Or was it the smell of fresh bread wafting down the creek bottom that drew him? Anyway, he hung around long enough to claim the crust, rock little Tod in adoring arms, and go home packing his own hot bread loaf in a brown paper bag.

After dinner (not "lunch," certainly) of pork chops from the freezer and pickled beets and pears from the cellar, I had a few more "sips" of *Dandelion Wine*, and that nearly forgotten indulgence, an afternoon nap. I woke at 3:30 to realize I'd missed the baby's bath.

"I like to wait until Ron comes in. He enjoys helping with the bath," Jane had told me. A pity to have missed this six-foot-five giant bathing his infant son. Cheers for the liberated generation of farmers.

My mother grew up along the banks of the Maumee River, and so it stirs in me the sort of longings the Jews harbor for Zion. At four o'clock I put on my blizzard gear and set a course for the river, stopping by the milking parlor to be certain they could manage without me. It appeared that they could. The Holsteins fixed me with apathetic stares, and I left.

Climbing the gate that let me into the pasture, I picked a path through the drifts to the edge of the creek and followed along the frozen stream to where it lost itself in the abundant open waters of the swift Maumee.

I put an arm around a sycamore tree and leaned there a while dreaming, watching for Indians to slip past in canoes. From up the river came a honking of geese, and four graceful swimming birds were joined by ten more fluttering down to the water, great wings flapping. They glided by with the gathering ice floes just as they had glided past the little girl watching from an Ohio thicket on the Maumee eighty years ago, just as they had glided past the silent Indians, past the troops of Mad Anthony Wayne a long century earlier.

I made my way back to the house, the afternoon ended, and the quiet waters of that special day flowed on into the mainstream of my life.

Retrospective

Teddy's birthday was on Sunday this year, as on the year he was born. His good friends gathered in the early morning hours and drank his health as they always had. We put twenty-two red carnations on the altar to commemorate his life. Teddy died four months ago.

The words "Teddy died" still leap out and startle me. It is as though they had been written in lemon juice to be revealed by the burning candle of time. But we can say them, and we do—often, for they divide all time for us. Everything is "before Teddy died," or "after . . ."

I would have thought it insupportable to lose a child. But it is not. I have watched other parents go through this and asked myself how they endured. I still ask. Each time I round the bend on Gifford Road that leads past the Beyer house, I think of pretty little Bonnie who died two years ago. "How does her mother go on?"

The paradox is that I only think of Ruth Beyer in terms of her loss. I don't immediately see her as a woman devoted to other children, busy with her house and farm and animals—nor do I see her as she sees herself, as I see myself.

In the final analysis it is the quality of our lives that equips us to cope or consigns us to despair in this sort of tragedy. Paul and I have much to sustain us.

People seem to repeat an old cliché when a child dies: "It doesn't matter if you have other children or not. It's no easier."

We find that it does matter—very much. I keep wanting to encourage young couples to "have another child. Have three! Have four! What if . . . ?" Dane and Orrin take on expanded roles in our lives, and we cherish them with new awareness. And we cherish more deeply the other young people who share our lives—nieces, nephews, Ted's close friends. There is no lack of people on whom to lavish attention, and the love flows back to help fill the awful void.

But our sons were never our whole existence. We have a life that belongs to the two of us. And each of us has a life built on individual satisfactions. My own independent ventures, my writing and speaking, were not fraught without guilt. I worried that I had neglected Ted and Orrin in their high school and college years.

They said it was the making of their own independence. Now, in light of this tragedy in my life, I find myself telling young mothers, "Give yourself to the children during these young years of their lives, but save something for yourself. You never know. . . ."

Many people write books about grieving, and you can learn to grieve by the rules. I never could learn things from rules, so I rejected them and grieved after my own fashion. And I too can write rules now.

Most important, I have learned not to grieve for the long-ago child. Teddy was never going to be three or six or ten again. Those years of his life are as securely ours as the childhood years of our living sons.

At twenty-one, Ted's future was not going to belong to us as his earlier years had. We had hoped he'd come home to farm, but he had a lot of trails to ride first. And one of those pretty girls down the trail was going to nab him sooner or later.

Our grieving centers, rather, on the vibrant boy who lived in the now, entranced by a well-tuned engine, determined to be Number One trials motorcycle racer in the country. It no longer matters to us that his dreams were not our dreams. What matters is that we encouraged him to pursue his. We miss his good looks, wit, the sense of excitement he brought to our lives.

I think our suffering climaxed the afternoon of the day Ted died, when we walked up the lane and came upon his field of soybeans ripening in the late September sun—tangible evidence of the unharvested fruit of his aborted life. We sobbed together the deep, wracking sobs of the broken-hearted, the sobs that must come in the long interval before you accept the inevitable truth: Someone else will rise up to harvest the beans, to ride the trails, to marry the pretty girls, to fulfill the dreams.

Rocky Mountain High

There are a few legendary place names that stir dormant yearnings in almost everyone for reasons lost in the mists of one's conditioning: the Alhambra, the coast of Maine, the Vienna woods, the valley of the Nile.

With skiers there is a similar syndrome of response to fabled slopes: Little Nell, Hahnenkamm, K22, Big Burn, Kitzbühlerhorn—everybody knows them. If they haven't been there, the ski magazines have detailed the terrain, the lore. These famous trails are, in effect, a language all their own.

Ruthie's Run, mentioned in a crowd of skiers, triggers everyone's personal experience of Ajax Mountain's storied run at Aspen: year, companions, snow conditions, make of skis, wax—well, a lot more detail than anybody except the skier reflecting gives a hoot about. Nobody else is listening. He's engrossed in his own memories.

Mention the back bowls of Vail, and before anybody launches into reverie, there will be a communal sigh, then the avalanche of reminiscences. If you are the unbeliever who has not been to THE mountain, these conversations will bore you, but they do not escape you. You are drawn subliminally into the mystique.

I would have been intrigued by "the back bowls of Vail" even if I hadn't been a skier. There is a euphony about the words that provokes the imagination as a good book title does. Then one morning you ride the gondola up the face of Lion's Head, fumble with the ski map (ski trails at most areas are so extensive that, yes, you do need maps), bumble your way via various lifts to the summit, pole over the ridge, take a steep schuss and a long traverse, and at last stand on the rim of the back bowls of Vail.

Falling away beneath and beyond you in cupping meadows with deceptively gentle slopes are miles and miles of snow, broken only by the weathered pinnacles of a dead tree, a scattering of pine, a whisper of aspen. On the distant horizon another range of mountains, ancient, majestic, bears silent witness to your baptism in the faith.

There under a royal blue sky you drop down from that rim onto a sloping field of virgin snow, floating on the powder, a rooster tail of white fanning in your wake—"heaven above, heaven below" as Thoreau put it—this is what it's all about.

The miles to the mountain, the lost mittens, the raw place on the ankle, the ache through the shoulders, the tomfoolery with pants and parkas, poles and skis, the money melting away—the whole insane ordeal finds atonement in the religious exhilaration of this moment.

It's an exhilaration that doesn't occur every ski day; but it's heady, and it's contagious. It easily makes bums of the uncommitted, and condemns the otherwise rational to a lifelong quest for better snows.

Sellers' Market

Turn the key of the pickup and it goes, "Vroom, Vroom!" with a deep and promising roar. Put it in gear, and it leaps out like a greyhound from the gates. Sitting by the mailbox it idles in a satisfying hum. It says, "I'm paid for, I'm paid for, I'm paid for, I'm paid for."

Now take a look at 'er. A sorry sight, a derelict from a demolition derby. The fenders flap, the front bumper twists in a grimace. The rocker panels are filigree; the tailgate has been worked over by a shopful of FFA boys. One taillight is blind; an angry crack zigzags across the windshield.

You can't get any respect at a farm auction in a wreck like that. Over at the lumberyard they fix you with a jaundiced eye. There's only so much you can accomplish with baling wire and Bondo. So . . . rainy day, we're going out to the showrooms and kick a few tires. I've been through this before; I go fortified with new buttons to sew on an old coat.

We go around to Mike's Place. Mike looks very friendly on the TV ads.

"Help you?" says a young guy with red sideburns.

"Wanta buy a pickup," says the farmer.

"George is our pickup man," says Sideburns. "I'll send him out."

I sit down, thread a needle, snip off an old button. Paul wanders around, slams a few car doors, peers into the orange-carpeted interior of a "sin bin" painted with nudes skipping hand in hand through Nirvana. George walks through with coffee.

Paul reads brochures about trucks. I start on the second button. . . . Paul reads brochures about cars. I finish the third button. . . . George is very busy. Through a glass partition we see him talking animatedly with a secretary. We slam Mike's showroom door.

We drive to Ed's Place. "Ed wrote the book on pickups," it says in the paper. At Ed's we win Barry. Barry has already had his morning coffee. We go into the cubicle that has Barry's outstanding salesmanship certificates on the wall, Barry's wife and children on the desk, Barry's ashtray, and Barry's complicated phone. I start sewing on coat button number four.

"What do you want on this pickup?"

"Fenders . . . a motor . . . tires would be nice . . . a rear bumper. . . . You know, the usual stuff."

"We can get you just what you want. Give us a few weeks." He gives us a price, wants to see our trade-in. Among the sleek and shiny autos in Ed's parking lot our pickup looks like a fugitive from Ziebart. Barry looks at it as if he wishes it weren't there. We drive it away.

At Joe's Place we are introduced to Bob. Bob smokes too much and ends every statement with "Okay?" I am shaking my head over buttons numbers five, six, and seven: I refuse to agree with anybody who thinks everything is okay.

I affix buttons eight and nine. I recall the first time we bought a pickup. . . . An eager young guy drove a powder blue Studebaker up our road one noon while we were eating lunch. He came up on the porch, introduced himself, and called us all out. He opened the truck door and said, "Hop in and take a spin."

We piled in with our little kids, their eyes shining. Drove slowly down the road. Honked and waved, neighbors peeking from behind curtains saying, "WOW!"

Drove proudly home, parked. Walked around 'er, hands in pockets, salesman lifting the hood, all staring knowledgeably at the baffling array of wires, plugs, shiny black mysteries. We bought it, right off. . . .

We proceed next to Jim's Place. Jim's grandad sold a truck to our grandad. Jim's dad sold a truck to our dad. Jim wants to sell us a truck. What color do we want? Jim doesn't have a truck of any color, but he'll feed all the specs into an electronic brain, and in six or eight weeks, at the end of a computerized assembly line, will be a new Leimbach truck, candy apple red and ready—perhaps.

We're going to spend $9,000 for a truck, and we haven't set foot in a truck, haven't even seen a real one. I'm not sure I can open the door with my crooked thumb. I can't tell from the picture whether I can reach the pedals or see over the hood. I have no way of knowing if it'll start, let alone how it rides or drives.

I cut the thread on button number ten, and we drive slowly home.

"Well, what do you think?" says Paul.

"I think that a battered truck that goes 'Vroom!' in the garage is worth ten in a computer any old day of the week," says I.

Modern Agrarian

There's a new building rising on the horizon to the north! On the tax duplicate we'll call it a machinery shed. On the computerized record system it's item number 20207 to be depreciated over a twelve-year period. It is, in fact, a pole barn with white steel siding, designed with sliding doors on two sides for easy access by tractors, wagons, sprayers, and so forth.

It lacks the charm of Pete Newberry's hip-roofed barn of the silvery, weathered siding that went to glory from that spot three years ago. (We bought the Newberry farm in the fifties, but by rural tradition it retains Pete's name.) It's totally devoid of personality, but it does symbolize a hope for the future. The principal barns at End o' Way date to the late nineteenth century, and most of them haven't seen paint since they were raised.

"Doesn't pay to paint a barn," was the cryptic assessment of

188

Grandpa Siebert. It was a judgment he had from his father and grand-father and passed to his son and grandson.

It took me fifteen years of nagging to get some red paint on the near sides of the barns visible from the kitchen window. "What's the use of painting them," Paul would say, "when they're all going to be replaced?" When I would suggest that we get on with the replace-ment, he would counter with, "A building doesn't make you any money," an aphorism I could trace through the same lineage as the remark about paint. It's always been a Catch-22 situation.

So the investment went instead into land and drain tile, machinery and fertilizer. Paul shored up an old barn with cement blocks, re-paired a roof here and there, poured a concrete floor to facilitate the use of pallets and forklifts, removed inconvenient partitions, and crowded his twentieth-century machinery in around the virgin oak timbers.

Now a new generation of Leimbachs have come on, unburdened by decades of debt and frugality, impatient of inconvenience, more influenced by the apparent well-being of other people's businesses. They come from the university with psychological conditioning to defeat their great-grandfather's adage. . . . "Gotta spruce up the place, get you a big office and a computer." And they add conditions of their own. "I'm not coming back here to farm if we don't build a decent machine shop"—that from Ted.

Last winter Paul and Orrin tore down the corncrib. They wanted to burn it, but I protested. "What! Burn all that barn siding and those beautiful beams!" In impatient compliance Paul stored them away in the "big barn," the oldest and biggest of the original structures. An assortment of old treasures handed down from the loft—antique milk cans, old baskets, and a sleigh among them—were relegated to the third floor of that same barn, secure against the foreseeable future.

I went away for two weeks in February, and when I returned, there, filling the shocking emptiness where the corncrib had stood, was a shiny red pole barn decked out with white shutters. It already had a measure of character because it was Ted's dream. Now we have this second building, this machinery shed, and I hear rumblings about a third, a potato barn—we already have one specially insulated barn for potatoes that was built in the sixties—to go out on the hillside where the machinery has been parked.

It's what I wanted, I guess. An air of prosperity is long overdue. But now I have weathered thirty years with those barns, and I see them as a link I don't want to lose. When the cousins come with their children to point out the haymow where they played, the place where the rope was tied, the basket loft, how sad to say, "Gone. . . ."

I've grown attached to the needleworks, sketches, paintings, and photographs of them that accumulate among our belongings. The "big barn" was the frontispiece chosen by the artist from the East who illustrated my first book, *A Thread of Blue Denim.*

"You'd have to be from Connecticut to appreciate that weatherbeaten wreck," says Paul.

I suppose he and Orrin will replace them one by one—the horse barn, the cow barn, the seed house, and so on. But the "big barn"? No, I don't think so. It's going to be crammed from floor to rafters with beams and barn siding, sleighs and bobsleds, old tables and rocking chairs, barrels and harness, antique tools and implements, shutters and milk stools, all jealously guarded by ghosts.

Christening Dress

It has finally been decided that, colic or no colic, Sarah must be christened. (Our granddaughter was born four months ago.) It's not the fear of original sin that's forcing the issue, but the fear that she may outgrow the christening dress.

So Grandma Pat has once more fished through those heavy, linen-closet drawers crammed with great bulks of seldom-used stuff and unearthed the yellowed box tied with a wrinkled, pink ribbon into which Great-grandmother Leimbach folded the dress so lovingly thirty-three years ago.

It's not without an ache in the heart that I unfold and admire it, as I have done at happy and not-so-happy intervals through the years. The lingering sorrow is that Grandma Lucy never saw a baby swaddled in this dress. Almost immediately that I was pregnant with Dane, she went to work on it—cut it from fine batiste and stitched it with tiny French seams in minute hand stitches as she had been properly taught to do at her mother's knee.

As an accomplished farm girl in the second decade of the century, Lucy went off for months at a time to sew whole wardrobes for women of ample means. She later studied at Michigan Normal School, joining the vanguard of teachers who were to transform the household arts into "domestic science."

Everyone who knew Lucy Leimbach remembers her sitting calm and erect wherever she was, her fingers moving swiftly and skillfully with her silver tatting shuttle. She worked her very finest tatting to edge the ruffles at the neck and sleeves of our baby's christening dress, then set in a broad, intricate band of the delicate stuff just above the wide hem.

She was an undemonstrative woman, and she didn't bubble over about her accomplishment (as I would have), but I have had years to consider what delight she must have taken in the project—this dear little dress, and the matching petticoat, also edged in tatting and fastened with tiny buttons and handworked buttonholes.

When Dane was born, and the christening date arrived, Paul and I decided in our foolish, immature way that a boy really shouldn't be christened in a dress. And, lady that she was, Lucy yielded to our decision without the slightest hint of disappointment. It was nothing to us; there would, of course, be a girl in a year or two who would wear the dress. I tucked the box away in the linen drawer, emptier then—like our heads!

But there came no little girl, nor any more little boys for many years. Lucy died, and part of my personal grief was that beautiful baby dress, folded away in its tissue paper like an old maid's trousseau.

When Teddy finally came as an answer to eight years of prayer, you may bet he wore the christening dress, as did Orrin who followed him. But it was too late for the splendid fulfillment belonging to the gifted lady who sewed it, that quarter hour after church on the christening day when all her circle ladies would have clustered about and taken envious note of her marvelous achievement.

Now Grandma Pat has it freshly laundered and pressed and ready for the holy day. As some sort of atonement perhaps, or a tribute at least, to Grandma Lucy's loving efforts, I have embroidered the broad hem of this dress with the names of those babies who have worn it, Paul Theodore, Orrin Alfred, and Sarah Caldwell, who will wear it tomorrow, as well as the name of the baby who never wore it —Dane Penton Leimbach.

Green Beer and Good Cheer

For several years the Northwest Airlines magazine carried a March feature in which it solicited comment from famous people on "favorite things Irish." The answers were as various as Yeats' grave, the quays of Dublin at sunset, and a recipe for Irish soda bread. It was a delightful article, punctuated with Emerald Island photographs of stone cottages, donkey carts, and old nuns sitting in the sun. It also fulfilled the challenge of any good piece of writing, it invited participation. . . .

My favorite thing Irish? Moe's Bar on St. Patrick's Day back in the late forties. Moe's was a grungy little dive at the foot of Mayfield Hill on Cleveland's east side just across Euclid Avenue and the streetcar tracks from the university.

Moe's was an unspeakably dirty graffiti palace lit by naked bulbs and smelling of smoke and beer and too-warm bodies. You could carve your initials in the grime on the tables if you made room among the ashtrays and beer glasses and stacks of textbooks. The walls were a penciled roster of fraternity symbols and fraternity men and their follies in those years of frivolous release following the war. (A pity it is that nobody preserved a wall from Moe's as a significant relic of the era.) It was the "in" place to socialize in a day when dormitory smoking was confined to designated rooms known as "smokers" and drinking anything alcoholic on campus was grounds for expulsion.

Moe's was the first and only bar that most of us knew. Here we had those first revolting swallows of beer and tried to persuade ourselves that it was good. Here in the white heat of peer pressure, many lost their battle with tobacco, and an unhappy few embraced the Epicurean philosophy altogether and flunked out.

It would be dishonest to paint myself as a member of the groovy "in" group who hung around Moe's. It was a role I secretly coveted but couldn't afford—temporally, ethically, or financially. But when winter lingered overlong and midterms called up suicide, a little St. Patrick's Day indulgence came as an Irish blessing.

Moe was probably as Irish as Fiorello La Guardia, but on St. Paddy's Day the Callahans and the Fitzgeralds and the O'Reilleys piled in from John Carroll, the Jesuit school in the Heights, and Moe's was an Irish pub. The singing was more than usually lusty, and the beer was green. As the evening wore on, the coeds took on a little of its

color. When the 3.2 percent was adding up to ten or fifteen, somebody would start the litany: "They're gonna tear down Moe's!"

"Booo. . . ."

"Gonna build a bigger one!"

"Yaaay. . . ."

"Only one bar!"

"Booo. . . ."

"Ninety feet long!"

"Yaaay. . . ."

"Not gonna sell beer!"

"Booo. . . ."

"Gonna give it away!"

"Yaaay. . . ."

"Only one bartender!"

"Booo. . . ."

"Ninety-nine barmaids!"

"Yaaay. . . ."

It went on raucously for a while, petering out finally when somebody
struck up a chorus of "The Night That Paddy Murphy Died."

At 12:45 we would lollygag back to campus, laughing or singing
boisterously, being sure to press the dorm buzzer before the 1:00
curfew, being careful not to breathe on the housemother. Hurrah for
the Irish and their talent for lifting the heart.

And whatever happened to Moe's, that good, old, sometimes Irish
pub? They tore it down, built a bigger one, and tried to keep it clean.
Evin the divil deserted the place.

Epitaph for Minnie

My sister Mary and I went one mild March afternoon to sit with the
mourners at Minnie Sabiers' funeral. Minnie was one of those little
maiden ladies you wondered at—pretty, pleasant, industrious. How
was she overlooked? Some sad fate of that heroic first war? Overpro-
tective parents? Simple independence? Her passing at eighty-six
shook the town no more than her life, but it did call up for Mary and
me a syndrome of what village life had been in that benign era between wars when we were children.

Our parents had a sort of "apple arrangement" with Doc Schaeffer, good friend and village dentist. He fixed nine sets of teeth in exchange for apples, cider, peaches, cherries, asparagus—whatever grew at Penton Orchards. It was a barter system built of pride and dignity and devoid of tax implication.

Minnie Sabiers was Doc Schaeffer's "nurse" before the specialists coined the term "dental technician." As such she played a merciful role in the continuing drama of terror staged in the dental offices up over the bank in downtown Amherst. Her quiet, antiseptic presence, her cool touch, her soothing words always promised that eventually the hot bur would cease its drilling and that Doctor Bill would reach up, push away the Rube Goldberg drill linkage, and call out, "One amalgam, Minnie."

Then he would hoist an enormous foot onto the windowsill, lean his elbow on his long, spare knee, and peer down onto the intersection of Park Avenue and Church Street while Minnie kneaded the amalgam on her soft, white palms. Ah, those ministering hands that stand out like rainbows from the myriad details of childhood. Here was a moment of salvation to cling to out of the worst moments of life —when the drilling was done, and you sank exhausted and spent into the black leather cushions, aware suddenly that your feet were pleasantly elevated, your head comfortably supported, there were cotton candy clouds floating over Mayor Cooper's office across the street, and the huge cross section of tooth diagrammed and labeled on the wall ("The Healthy Tooth; The Decaying Tooth; The Aching Tooth; The Abscessed Tooth") could no longer intimidate you.

There was the pleasant scrunching then of the pliable amalgam into the enormous crater the tongue discovered and a flourish with some sort of scraping-shaping tool; Doctor Bill pushed back the white china tray strewn with the instruments of torture, depressed the pedal that lowered the chair in a soft "shoosh," swept off your white linen bib, and it was over. Then he would reach down into his pocket, pull out a handful of change, choose a nickel, and lay it in your sweaty hand. "There, tell your ma to stop by Baetz's Dairy and get you an ice cream cone."

When Doctor Bill retired and young Doctor Roy took over his office and his nurse, I became aware that "Minnie" had somehow become "Mollie." It seems that she had taken a late stand against a name she never liked. (Perhaps it had to do with connotations of Minnie Mouse, who rose to fame in the same era.)

None of us who had lain for tortured childhood hours in that little corner office above the bank were ever really at peace with the name change. But how could she have known that for us her name was a lifeline, that when all life's joy was suspended, when fear, pain, anguish held sway, when hope was at an ebb, annihilation near . . . then—out of the abyss—those life-sustaining words made hers the dearest name in all the world: "One amalgam, Minnie."

Considering the Christian hope to which Reverend VanderWyden assigned her that afternoon out at Ridgehill Cemetery, it occurred to Mary and me that they might have fit well into an epitaph for her headstone: "The Worst Is Past. One Amalgam, Minnie!"

In Memoriam

When my husband dismantled his mother's garden and replanted it to grass, he left a peck of narcissus and daffodil bulbs on the porch with the offhand suggestion that I "do something" with them. I planted them finally in the fringe of woods that runs along the river bluff on the Newberry place. A peck doesn't go far when you're dealing with a hundred acres of woods, but after ten years they're a nice surprise to the unsuspecting woods wanderer.

"Hey, Mom," said Dane one year. "There's a whole mess of daffodils just growing wild down there at the top of Newberry's dugway."

"Is that so?" said I.

Last fall I planted a few more, this time along the grass-grown trails where our Teddy used to ride his motorcycle. It may take me the rest of my life to do the whole distance, but it's nice to contemplate a golden memorial trail.

Last week Paul and I took a picnic lunch and went to check on the daffodils. We were ahead of the blooming, but we did do a spring inventory. In a sheltered gully beneath the hill the skunk cabbage unfurled their great shiny leaves with a flourish that would be unremarkable in the oblivion of a green June. The May apples skewered their way through the leaf mulch, but not much more than the daffodil spikes have broken dormancy on these high, windy bluffs.

"There's still a lot of water under that rye," said Paul. (Which translates as, "Too early to plow.")

"Best stand of rye we've had in many a year," he mused.

"That's because I planted it," said I.

"That was wheat you planted. Crookedest darned rows I ever saw."

"You know what they say," I jested, "get more grain in a crooked row than a straight one."

"Tell that to the fellow who runs the combine!"

We had our lunch in an ash grove looking across our wooded kingdom and down a hundred and fifty feet to the river, swollen now with the last of the spring snow runoff. The dogs, watchful sleuths that they are, had followed along. Heidi, smelling strongly of early morning woodchuck, lay at a merciful distance on a bed of dead leaves, pillowed her head on a stone, and slept. Thatcher had to be reminded that it wasn't his party, and that he should get his eager nose out of the picnic bag. He scratched a shallow depression then among the tree roots and nestled his hot body against the cool earth, waiting patiently for what scraps we tendered.

"When will you plant the peas?" I asked, taking up the conversation of a half hour earlier, the way folks do who know each other's silences.

"As soon as the rain passes. The drainage channels are already established through the ground cover. If I'd plowed it, it wouldn't drain as quickly. Anyhow, the ground is still cold. A warm rain'll help."

Rain! The sun was shining on our picnic and I'd never given a thought to rain, but to the farmer it was a given. He'd been up early to catch the weather map, but even without that he read rain on the horizon, felt it in the air. As if we had summoned moisture by speaking of it, a cloud cover moved across the sky, a breeze sprang up, and a chill moved up from the river. ("You know how it is with an April day . . .")

We folded our blanket, collected our gear, and hurried down the lane to the house as a few drops of rain began to spit in the wind.

"This will be the greening rain," said Paul. "Day after tomorrow we'll plant the peas, and Ted's daffodils will bloom."

CHRISTIAN HERALD
People Making A Difference

Christian Herald is a family of dedicated, Christ-centered ministries that reaches out to deprived children in need, and to homeless men who are lost in alcoholism and drug addiction. Christian Herald also offers the finest in family and evangelical literature through its book clubs and publishes a popular, dynamic magazine for today's Christians.

Our Ministries

Family Bookshelf and **Christian Bookshelf** provide a wide selection of inspirational reading and Christian literature written by best-selling authors. All books are recommended by an Advisory Board of distinguished writers and editors.

Christian Herald magazine is contemporary, a dynamic publication that addresses the vital concerns of today's Christian. Each monthly issue contains a sharing of true personal stories written by people who have found in Christ the strength to make a difference in the world around them.

Christian Herald Children. The door of God's grace opens wide to give impoverished youngsters a breath of fresh air, away from the evils of the streets. Every summer, hundreds of youngsters are welcomed at the Christian Herald Mont Lawn Camp located in the Poconos at Bushkill, Pennsylvania. Year-round assistance is also provided, including teen programs, tutoring in reading and writing, family counseling, career guidance and college scholarship programs.

The Bowery Mission. Located in New York City, the Bowery Mission offers hope and Gospel strength to the downtrodden and homeless. Here, the men of Skid Row are fed, clothed, ministered to. Many voluntarily enter a 6-month discipleship program of spiritual guidance, nutrition therapy and Bible study.

Our Father's House. Located in rural Pennsylvania, Our Father's House is a discipleship and job training center. Alcoholics and drug addicts are given an opportunity to recover, away from the temptations of city streets.

Christian Herald ministries, founded in 1878, are supported by the voluntary contributions of individuals and by legacies and bequests. Contributions are tax deductible. Checks should be made out to Christian Herald Children, The Bowery Mission, or to Christian Herald Association.

Administrative Office: 40 Overlook Drive, Chappaqua, New York 10514
Telephone: (914) 769-9000

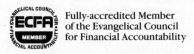 Fully-accredited Member
of the Evangelical Council
for Financial Accountability